# SIMPLY MODERN

# WEDDING CAKES

## LINDY SMITH

**D&C**
David and Charles

www.stitchcraftcreate.co.uk

# CONTENTS

## LEFT TO RIGHT FROM TOP:

Glitz and Glamour, Sweetheart Stripes, Designer Doodle Art, Radiant Ribbons, Fabulous Fringes, Something Blue, Summertime Blooms, Flamboyant Fleur-de-lis, Retro Circles, Bridal Vogue.

# INTRODUCTION

*Wedding* cakes are very special and it's a real privilege to be asked to create such an important centrepiece. I have worked with many wonderful couples over the years who have sparked my imagination and have had the confidence to be adventurous. I find dreaming up concepts and designs and then creating one-of-a-kind wedding cakes both extremely thrilling and rewarding.

Research for this book has taken me right around the world, as wedding cake styles and trends are now more global than they have ever been before. I've discovered some wonderful new techniques and a number of interesting ideas. The book has evolved and changed as it has been created, but I am really happy with the finished result. I hope you find the collection inspiring and that it enables you to create your own dream wedding cake.

Wedding cakes are the pinnacle of the cake world – the ultimate cake decorating challenge – so it is not surprising that many people find the prospect of creating such an important cake a little daunting. I hope that by reading through the introduction section and familiarizing yourself with the basics at the back of the book that you will gain the confidence to create or adapt my designs and ideas, whether you are a first-time cake decorator or a qualified professional.

As always, I love to see how I've inspired you, so please do add pictures of your creations to Pinterest, quoting my name or this book so I can easily find them, tweet on Twitter using my handle @LindysCakes or post onto the Lindy's Cakes Facebook page.

To see more of my designs and to look for cake inspiration please visit my website, where you will find a wealth of examples just waiting for you to discover. Click on the galleries, the blog and the shop to see cakes in all shapes, sizes and colours. Please also note that all the specialist equipment and tools that you will need to create the cakes in this book are available via the shop on my website.

I hope you find this book an inspiration.

Happy sugarcrafting!

*Lindy Smith*

**WWW.LINDYSCAKES.CO.UK**

# DREAMING AND PLANNING

A wedding cake is one of the classic elements of a wedding reception, but when choosing the look and style of your design, it's definitely not necessary to be traditional. Today, more than ever before, there is a plethora of possibilities: wedding cakes can be created in any colour scheme and in all shapes and sizes, ranging from beautifully chic and simple to incredibly complex and extravagant creations. From meeting many brides, I know the choice can be overwhelming, so I have listed a few pointers to get you thinking:

# Things to consider

## YOUR STYLE

It may be obvious, but everyone's taste and style is different: what appeals to one person may not necessarily appeal to the next. Choosing a cake is all about what feels right to you.

You may find it helpful to create a moodboard of pictures that you feel drawn to: I have included a moodboard at the start of each project to show you what helped inspire me to create each design. These don't necessarily have to be images of wedding cakes or bridal inspirations; they can include everyday items, such as gorgeous cushions or sumptuous fabrics, photos of somewhere really special to you, the latest haute couture fashion range that you think is fantastic, the amazing natural world or even the work of an artist you admire. Use either an old-fashioned pinboard or websites, such as Pinterest, to help you organize your ideas. The process of creating a moodboard will help you narrow down your choices and assist with prioritizing; it will probably inspire more ideas but ultimately it will enable your dream wedding cake to start to take shape.

## THE VENUE

Wedding venues – like wedding cakes – vary enormously, from wonderful medieval stone castles to gorgeous open-air marquees set in beautiful scented gardens. They can include sophisticated city hotels, delightful vintage village halls and sunny beaches. Your venue can be an important influence when choosing the design of your wedding cake. For example, I added decorations on thin wires to a cake I designed and created for a couple whose reception was on a moving boat; the gentle movement of the boat meant that the decorations 'danced' around the top of the cake – delightful!

Your venue is important, however, don't think that because your reception is in a stately home, for example, that you can't opt for a modern cake. A modern design that reflects your style can look simply stunning centre stage in a grand ballroom or positioned by a sweeping staircase.

## COLOUR

Your wedding colours can help to set the style, atmosphere and mood of your celebration. Most brides these days choose a colour palette from which to theme their weddings. Although white is still very much the predominant colour for bridal gowns – a fashion credited to Queen Victoria – gone are the days when the cake has to be all white too.

Colours – like fashions – come and go, so my recommendation is that you select colours that appeal to you. Think about the colours and patterns that you surround yourself with, look in your wardrobe and around your home and use the shades you find as a starting point. Your wedding colour scheme can also be inspired by your wedding venue or the time of year.

It is a good idea to check that your chosen colour palette works in your venue. Clashing palettes aren't good – I once made a delicate lilac wedding cake for a lilac-themed wedding, only to discover when I delivered the cake that it was to be displayed against red and gold flock wallpaper!

## THEME

Having a theme can help you focus. Your theme can be dictated by your chosen colours, a significant flower, an era or even your venue's own style. It can be as simple as a country-themed wedding or as glamorous and over-the-top as an opera-inspired celebration. Whatever theme you choose, your wedding cake can be created to complement it. Alternatively, it can be designed to stand alone as a personalized centrepiece of edible art to amaze and delight your guests – the choice is yours!

## SIZE OF VENUE AND GUEST LIST

Obviously, the more guests you invite, the more cake you will need. However, it is not necessary to have all the cake on show, as iced cutting cakes behind the scenes can help feed large numbers without the need for creating a very large, multi-tiered wedding cake. If, on the other hand, you have a small, intimate wedding in a venue that calls out for a tall cake, simply use polystyrene cake dummies for some of the tiers.

I have suggested sponge cake serving numbers for all the projects in this book. However, to help you adapt my designs and work out how much cake you will need, I have included a cake portion guide below. The number of portions cut from a cake depends on whether the cake cuts cleanly and the dexterity of the person cutting the cake. The cake portions on the chart have been based on 7.5cm (3in) deep cakes; with fruit cake cut into 2.5cm (1in) square slices and sponge cakes – which are served in larger portions – cut into 5 × 2.5cm (2 × 1in) slices. Many caterers do cut smaller than this, so your cake will go a lot further. However, I find it is always better to overestimate the number of portions required.

*Note: if it is to be served as a dessert, you will need to halve the number of portions cut from each sponge cake.*

### ROUGH GUIDE TO PORTIONS

To work out roughly how many portions can be cut from a cake of any size, simply divide the volume of a standard portion into the volume of a completed cake. I find a spreadsheet is very useful.

| CAKE SIZE | | | APPROXIMATE PORTIONS FOR 7.5CM (3IN) DEEP CAKES | |
|---|---|---|---|---|
| Round and petal | Square and hexagon (measured side to side) | Ball | Fruit cake 2.5cm (1in) square slices | Sponge cake 5 × 2.5cm (2 × 1in) slices |
| 7.5cm (3in) | | | 9 | 4 |
| 10cm (4in) | 7.5cm (3in) | 10cm (4in) | 12 | 6 |
| 12.5cm (5in) | 10cm (4in) | | 16 | 8 |
| 15cm (6in) | 12.5cm (5in) | 12.5cm (5in) | 24 | 12 |
| 18cm (7in) | 15cm (6in) | | 34 | 17 |
| 20cm (8in) | 18cm (7in) | 15cm (6in) | 46 | 24 |
| 23cm (9in) | 20cm (8in) | | 58 | 28 |
| 25.5cm (10in) | 23cm (9in) | | 70 | 35 |
| 28cm (11in) | 25.5cm (10in) | | 95 | 47 |
| 30.5cm (12in) | 28cm (11in) | | 115 | 57 |
| 33cm (13in) | 30.5cm (12in) | | 137 | 68 |
| 35.5cm (14in) | 33cm (13in) | | 150 | 75 |

## SHAPE AND TIER SIZE OPTIONS

The shape of your cake is very much a personal choice, but it will no doubt be influenced by current wedding cake trends. You will see from the cakes I have designed for this book that I'm currently drawn to circular cakes, but by all means be more adventurous: cake tins are available in various shapes, including petals and hexagons, which work well as an integral part of a wedding cake design. Square cakes are also an option, and often caterers prefer this shape as they are easier to cut up and serve.

The height of your tiers is another consideration. Until recently, the standard depth of a UK wedding cake tier was 7.5cm (3in). However, over the last decade-and-a-half, wedding cake design has been influenced by global cake trends and tall, double-height-plus column cakes have become popular. I love using these tall cakes in my designs, as they add grace and elegance, without making the cake itself too big. These cakes also have the advantage of adding a large surface area for detailed design elements, as seen on the Flamboyant Fleur-de-lis and Glitz and Glamour cakes.

My advice is to experiment with shapes and sizes by using cake tins, polystyrene cake dummies and cake boards to see which shapes and sizes appeal and work for you. Be aware that the photos in this book can be deceptive: some cakes are fairly small, whilst others are actually quite large. Reconstructing the designs in cake dummies will convey an idea of their impact. If you wish to upscale, downscale or adapt any of my designs, using dummies in the first instance is also an excellent way of checking that the new proportions are still pleasing to the eye.

## ROUNDED OR SHARP TOP EDGES

For many years, rounded edges on sugarpaste (rolled fondant)-covered cakes were the norm in the UK, however a trend for sharp edges, which I first saw in Australia in 2009, has been steadily growing. There are various ways of achieving these edges, which are covered at the back of the book (see Covering Cakes with Sugarpaste).

I usually find that rather than having to choose one edge over another, the design of the cake itself often dictates the type of edge that is appropriate for each tier. I often mix and match the edge style on my cakes, but if you prefer one above the other, by all means adapt accordingly.

# Setting the scene

## POSITION

The cutting of the wedding cake by the bride and groom is the symbolic first task that newlyweds accomplish together, so it's important that the cake is positioned in an attractive, prominent place that creates a natural photo opportunity: a place where the wedding guests can easily see and marvel at the design before it is cut. I can't stress enough how important this is, so please ask your venue for suggestions and research your options.

Sometimes even what seems an obvious position has its drawbacks. I once set up a wedding cake in a beautiful ornate building with marble pillars and alcoves. The cake was positioned in front of one of these alcoves, which contained a statue of a Greek god. I thought all was perfect, until I received pictures afterwards – the cake looked wonderful, as did the bride and groom, but the focal point of the photo was the statue's genitalia framed behind the couple!

## LIGHTING

A wedding cake is one of the most photographed elements of a wedding – second to the bride – so think about lighting. Ensure your cake is well lit, for example under a spotlight or near a window. If the lighting isn't ideal, consider bringing in additional lights, as they will make all the difference.

## CAKE TABLE

Another consideration is the table or trolley on which the cake will sit. Size here is all-important; you don't want your cake to be dwarfed by a large table, or positioned on a table so small that it is in danger of being knocked. Try to ensure that the table is in proportion to the size of your cake.

The cake table can be left uncovered: elegant, polished or distressed rustic tables can complement a wedding cake beautifully. However, this is not always the case. If you plan to cover your table, think carefully – you want to enhance your cake rather than distract the eye away from it. A fine linen tablecloth may be perfect, but a predominantly white cake on a white tablecloth can become rather lost, so use coloured fabrics or linens to help make your cake pop.

## CAKE STAND

A cake stand – although not absolutely essential – lifts the cake away from the table surface, adds a touch of elegance and finishes off the design beautifully. Throughout this book I have used a selection of pedestal-type stands to give my designs a modern, cutting-edge feel. These stands are becoming more and more widely available and can be easily sourced over the Internet.

If you prefer something a little more traditional, you may find that your venue or caterer has a choice of beautiful, often antique, polished silver stands that you can use. Alternatively, think outside the box. I have seen wedding cakes displayed beautifully on piles of books, a wooden wine box, suitcases and glass platforms.

### THE SUN MOVES!

Ensure you keep your cake out of direct sunlight; it can only take a matter of minutes for some edible colours to fade and lose their vibrancy in strong light.

# SWEETHEART STRIPES

## SERVES 75

*This* colourful, three-tiered creation with its candy stripes, polka dots and ruffles is wonderfully flamboyant and fun, yet tasteful and sophisticated at the same time. The pink and peach shades complement each other exquisitely, standing out against the crisp, white sugarpaste (rolled fondant) covering. The ombre colours of the romantic ruffles on the base are perfect to balance the lightness of the polka-dot top tier, while the statement stripes embellishing the middle tier connect the two beautifully. The single playful heart in the centre of the design creates a wonderful focal point; ideal for a wedding, of course, as the universally recognized symbol of true love.

This lovely design incorporates three main elements: spots, stripes and ruffles. To make the spots for the top tier, I used a polka dot embosser to emboss the soft paste covering and to cut out spots from coloured modelling paste to fill. I made the scallops and heart feature on the middle tier using cutters, and cut the stripes with a multi-ribbon cutter. The ruffles were created using my moghal arch cutter and a cutting wheel. I then fluted the edges with a ball tool and gathered the shapes, before attaching them closely in colourful rows on the bottom tier, and onto a modelling paste ball to create a gorgeous pompom topper.

# You will need

## CAKES

Bake, layer and stack your choice of cakes to create the following tier sizes:

★ **base tier:** 20cm (8in) round, 9.5cm (3¾in) deep

★ **second tier:** 15cm (6in) round, 19cm (7½in) deep

★ **top tier:** 10cm (4in) round, 9cm (3½in) deep

## MATERIALS

★ **sugarpaste (rolled fondant):** 1.1kg (2lb 7oz) strong pink; 100g (3½oz) mid peach; 1.4kg (3lb 1½oz) white

★ **modelling paste:** 200g (7oz) each of seven shades, from strong pink through to peach (see Colours); 25g (1oz) white

★ 25g (1oz) white royal icing

★ sugar glue

## EQUIPMENT

★ **cake boards:** 28cm (11in) round cake drum; round hardboards the same size as each cake

★ 6cm (2⅜in) round × 1.5cm (⅝in) deep polystyrene round cake spacer, or 4 × 6 × 0.3cm (1½ × 2⅜ × ⅛in) hardboards

★ **cutters:** polka dot embosser (PC); multi-sized ribbon cutter (FMM); Lindy's round scallop cutter for a 15cm (6in) circle (LC); set of large heart cutters: 4.5–7.5cm (1¾–3in) wide; Lindy's moghal arch cutter (LC)

★ **dowels:** at least 20cm (8in) in length

★ scriber or pin

★ 1mm (¹⁄₃₂in) spacers

★ greaseproof (wax paper)

★ pearl-headed dressmakers' pin

★ smoother

★ set square

★ card

★ palette knife

★ craft knife

★ cutting wheel (PME)

★ foam pad

★ ball tool

★ wooden barbecue skewer

★ 90cm (35½in) length of 1.5cm (⅝in) wide pink velvet ribbon

★ non-toxic glue stick

## COLOURS

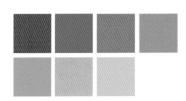

All the colours used on the cake were created using a mixture of the pretty pink sugarpaste (MT), plus Ruby (SF) and Marigold (SK) paste colours.

## SEAMLESS JOIN

The ruffles will cover the join in the paste created when covering the cake drum.

## RELEASE THE DOTS

If the dots are not released easily from the cutter, simply use a scriber or pin to help to remove them.

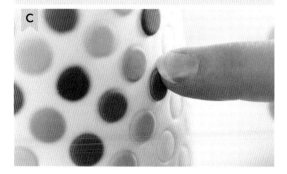

# Covering the cakes and board

**1.** Cover each of the cakes in turn (see Covering Cakes with Sugarpaste) as follows. Place the base tier centrally on the 28cm (11in) cake drum and cover the cake with strong pink sugarpaste using Method 1. Next cover the board by rolling out the trimmings into a long strip, cutting one edge straight and placing it onto the cake drum with the cut edge against the cake. Trim to size. Use Method 5 to cover the second tier with white sugarpaste, covering the top first followed by the sides. Cover the sides of the polystyrene spacer with mid peach sugarpaste using Method 3.

**2.** Cover the top tier with white sugarpaste using Method 1, then immediately emboss polka dots around the sides of the cake. To do this, place one end of the polka dot embosser vertically against the side of the cake and carefully, but firmly, press the embosser into the soft paste. Without releasing the pressure, use a rocking action to emboss the circles from one end of the embosser to the other onto the sides of the cake **(A)**. Remove the embosser and realign so the pattern is continuous, then press and rock as before. Continue until the polka dots completely cover the sides of the cake.

**3.** Dowel the base tier and middle tier (see Dowelling Cakes).

# Decorating the cakes

## TOP TIER

**1.** Using 1mm (1/32in) spacers, roll out a small amount of each of the seven modelling paste colours. Cut out a series of dots from each colour using the polka dot embosser **(B)**.

**2.** Attach the polka dots in a random colour pattern over the embossed dots on the cake sides using sugar glue. Smooth down the cut edges of each dot with a finger as you secure them in place **(C)**.

**3.** Roll out a strip of mid peach modelling paste between 1mm (1/32in) spacers and use a multi-sized ribbon cutter to cut out a 36 × 0.5cm (14¼ × ¼in) strip. Attach this strip to the base of the cake for a neat finish.

## MIDDLE TIER

### THE SCALLOPS

**1.** Make a 15cm (6in) diameter round paper template from greaseproof (wax) paper. Fold the circle into quarters and unfold: the centre of your circle will be where the folds meet. Place the template on top of the cake and mark the centre with a dressmakers' pin, as shown **(D)**.

**2.** Thinly roll out the pink, peach and light peach modelling paste between 1mm (¹⁄₃₂in) spacers for the circular top and scallop pattern. Use the round scallop cutter to cut out 14 pink, 8 peach and 7 light peach shapes from the pastes **(E)**.

**3.** Attach the cut out shapes so the scallops hang down at the same height around the edge of the cake and the triangular sections meet centrally on top **(F)**, referring to **(G)** for the colour sequence. Straighten the edges of each triangle on top of the cake, as necessary, using a straight edge or ruler. Once complete, run a smoother over the top of the cake for a smooth, uniform finish.

### THE STRIPES

**1.** Use a set square and a scriber to mark vertical placement lines onto the side of the cake. To do this, place the set square in line with the join between two scallops, scribe a 13.5cm (5¼in) high vertical line up from the base and repeat for all remaining scallops **(H)**.

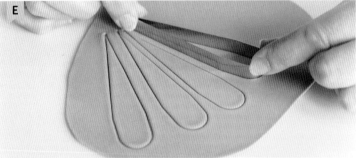

### SPACERS ESSENTIAL

Use spacers when rolling out your modelling paste to ensure an even thickness to your scallops, giving a smooth top to your cake.

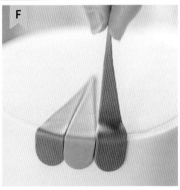

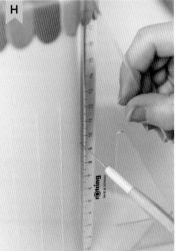

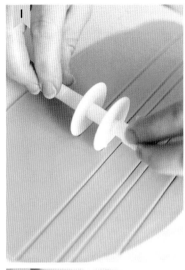

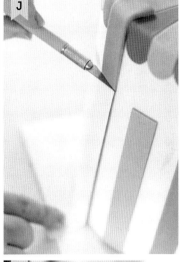

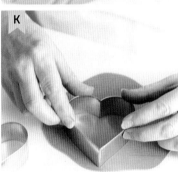

### PERFECT HEART

For a professional finish, take care when stacking your hearts to keep each one centrally aligned.

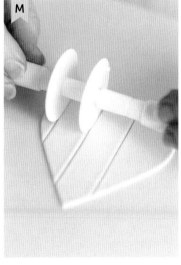

**2.** Roll out the peach and light peach modelling paste for the stripes on the sides of the cake between 1mm (¹⁄₃₂in) spacers. Set the multi-sized ribbon cutter to a 1.8cm (¾in) width and cut out seven stripes of each colour, at least 14cm (5½in) in length **(I)**.

**3.** Cut a 13.5cm (5¼in) long rectangle from card to use as a template for cutting. Attach the stripes between the scribed lines below the matching coloured scallops using sugar glue. Using the rectangular template and a craft knife, cut away the excess paste **(J)**.

### THE HEART MOTIF

**1.** Thinly roll out five shades of modelling paste between the 1mm (¹⁄₃₂in) spacers. Use the heart cutter set to cut out five hearts of varying sizes, referring to **(K)** for colour choices.

**2.** Lift the hearts with a palette knife and stack them in order of size – you will not need to add any sugar glue as the hearts will adhere to each other **(L)**.

**3.** Thinly roll out some white modelling paste between the 1mm (¹⁄₃₂in) spacers and cut out a heart to match the size of the largest modelling paste heart. Using the multi-sized ribbon cutter on the 1.8cm (¾in) width setting, cut a central vertical strip into the heart. Remove the cutter and reposition it so one edge is in the same cutting line as for the first cut, and then cut a second strip. Repeat on the other side of the heart **(M)**.

**4.** Attach the two outer white strips (those to either side of the central heart strip) to either side of one of the coloured strips on the cake, as shown **(N)**.

**5.** Attach the prepared stacked heart over the top of this area using sugar glue **(O)**. Trim away any excess white paste, as necessary, using a craft knife. Once in position, add a peach modelling paste polka dot to the top of the central pink heart.

**6.** Finally, roll out a thin strip of white sugarpaste, at least 53cm (21in) in length, between 1mm (¹⁄₃₂in) spacers. Set the multi-sized ribbon cutter to the 5mm (¼in) width setting and cut out one long and one short strip. Starting at the centre above the heart, attach the long strip horizontally around the top of the vertical strips. Cut the short strip to a length of 11cm (4¼in) and make a bow by bringing the ends of the strip into the centre to form two loops. Wrap a further short length around the centre to represent the knot. Allow the bow to firm up a little before attaching it in place on the cake with sugar glue.

## BASE TIER

**1.** Roll out some strong pink modelling paste between the 1mm (¹⁄₃₂in) spacers. Cut arches in the paste using the moghal arch cutter, leaving space beneath each one to complete the shape **(P)**.

**2.** Run a cutting wheel in a slight curve from one side of each arch to the other, to create uniform shapes **(Q)**.

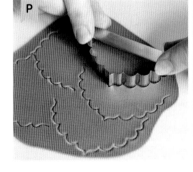

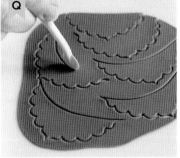

**3.** Place the shapes on a foam pad. Frill the fluted edges by pressing down on the paste with the larger end of a ball tool and stroking it repeatedly back and forth. The edges of the paste will thin and cup slightly, giving it movement **(R)**.

**4.** Pick up one frilled shape and pleat it approximately four times with your fingers, as shown in **(S)** and **(T)**. Once you have made the folds, pinch the base to create a gathered frill or ruffle **(U)** and repeat for the remaining frilled shapes.

**5.** Paint sugar glue over the lower section of the base tier and stick the 'stems' of the ruffles onto the cake, resting the first layer on the covered board.

**6.** Continue making and attaching ruffles in the same way, changing colour approximately every two or three rows, until you reach the top of the tier **(V)**.

**7.** Attach the decorated middle tier to the centre of the base tier using royal icing. Then continue to add the ruffles **(W)** until they rest vertically against the middle tier and the covered cake is no longer visible.

## RUFFLE SHUFFLE

Experiment with the cutters in your tool box to see what other types of ruffles you can make!

### SUGAR POMPOM TOPPER

**1.** Roll a 2cm (¾in) diameter ball of modelling paste and insert a wooden barbecue skewer into it. Make strong pink ruffles (see Base Tier, Steps 1–4) and secure their bases onto the ball by applying a very small amount of sugar glue onto each ruffle **(X)** – too much and they will slide!

**2.** Continue adding ruffles as shown **(Y)** until the pompom is complete. You might find it easier to cover the ball in stages, allowing sections to dry before moving on. Leave the pompom to dry completely.

## Assembling the cake

**1.** Using royal icing, attach the polystyrene spacer to the centre of the middle tier, then attach the polka dot top tier centrally to the top of the spacer, checking alignment and levels.

**2.** Attach the pink ribbon to the edge of the cake board using the non-toxic glue stick.

**3.** Remove the skewer from the pompom by gently twisting it until it releases. Add the dried sugar pompom once the cake is on display, using a touch of royal icing to secure it.

### PLAN AHEAD

Make the pompom in advance to allow the paste to dry thoroughly.

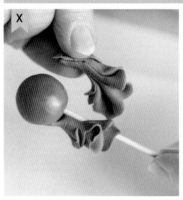

### QUICK DRY

To speed up the drying process, use a cool oven set at around 50–60°C (122–140°F) to quickly remove moisture from the modelling paste.

# Polka Dot Cookies

Bake heart-shaped cookies, cover with white sugarpaste and experiment with the polka dots, layered hearts, bows and ruffles used for the main cake to decorate. They make the perfect wedding favours to wow your guests.

# SOMETHING BLUE

### SERVES 60

**Something** old, something new, something borrowed... and this stylish cake is the perfect something blue! Tiled patterns and designs are fascinating in the way that they add interest and colour to often quite neutral spaces. This cake was partly inspired by a visit to the Royal Alcazar of Seville; a magnificent palace richly adorned with beautifully shaped tiles in fabulous patterns and colours. Here, a blue colour palette gives a cool, yet sophisticated look to this contemporary wedding cake but this, of course, can easily be adapted to suit. The patterns on the tiles themselves may look intricate, but they are created quickly and easily using stencils.

The blue and white tiles are the focal point of this elegant design. I have used a range of stencils to emboss the patterned modelling paste tiles, then dusted over the little flowers and geometric patterns with food colour dusts to make them pop. I used two of my Moroccan tile sets to cut out slightly different-sized tiles for each tier, then attached the tiles in neat rows around the cake, mixing up the colours to add interest to the design. For a delicate finishing touch, I decorated the top of the base tier with a lace stick embosser before adding some pretty edible paper carnations.

# You will need

## CAKES

Bake, layer and stack your choice of cakes to create the following tier sizes:

★ **base tier:** 17.5cm (7in) round, 19cm (7½in) deep

★ **second tier:** 12.5cm (5in) round, 9.5cm (3¾in) deep

## MATERIALS

★ 1.7kg (3lb 12oz) white sugarpaste (rolled fondant)

★ **modelling paste:**
100g (3½oz) deep blue;
50g (1¾oz) bright blue;
50g (1¾oz) sky blue;
125g (4½oz) white

★ **dust food colours:** bright blue (SK Bluebell); dark blue (SK Gentian)

★ white vegetable fat (shortening)

★ edible metallic white lustre dust (SK Snowflake)

★ **edible wafer (rice) paper carnations:** in green and white, made from 8cm (3¼in) and 5cm (2in) scalloped circles (see Edible Paper Flowers)

★ sugar glue

## EQUIPMENT

★ **hardboards:** 17.5cm (7in) and 12.5cm (5in) round, the same size as each cake

★ **dowels:** at least 20cm (8in) in length

★ 1mm (¹⁄₃₂in) spacers

★ **stencils:** selection with a suitable pattern size. Lindy used: Lindy's cherry blossom – LC106 (LC); Lindy's Chinese floral circle – LC104 (LC); Lindy's Greek repeat pattern – LC102 (LC); Lindy's hexagon set – LC109 (LC); Lindy's wild hedgerow flowers set – LC203 (LC); gem pendant – C566 (DS); mini check – C487 (DS)

★ smoother

★ paint palette

★ selection of paintbrushes for dusting

★ board or portable mat

★ **cutters:** Lindy's Moroccan tile – large and medium sets (LC)

★ craft knife

★ set square

★ lace motif stick embosser set – 20 (HP)

## COLOURS

Lindy used Sailing Blue sugarpaste (MT) to make the deep blue modelling paste and Gentian paste food colour (SK) to colour the bright and sky blue modelling paste.

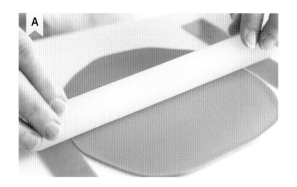

## SPACERS ESSENTIAL

It is important to use spacers to ensure that all your tiles are the same thickness.

# Covering and assembling the cakes

**1.** Place the top tier on the 12.5cm (5in) round hardboard, then use Method 1 to cover this cake with white sugarpaste (see Covering Cakes with Sugarpaste) and set aside.

**2.** Place the main cake on the 17.5cm (7in) round hardboard. Use Method 5 to cover this cake with sugarpaste, covering the top first followed by the sides, and set aside to dry.

**3.** Once the sugarpaste has set, dowel the base tier (see Dowelling Cakes). Securely place the top tier in position, checking that it is central and the cake is level.

# Decorating the cakes

## MAKING THE TILES

### BLUE-ON-DEEP BLUE TILES

**1.** Knead the deep blue modelling paste until it becomes warm and stretchy, then roll some of the paste out onto your work surface between 1mm (1/32in) spacers **(A)**.

**2.** Place the cherry blossom stencil on top of the modelling paste. Firmly press a smoother onto the stencil to force the modelling paste beneath it up to the top **(B)**.

**3.** Tip some of each of the dust food colours into a paint palette. Dip a paintbrush into one of the blue dusts, knock off any excess and carefully dust over some of the flowers and leaves of the stencil, varying the intensity of colour by adding more or less dust. Dip a clean paintbrush into the second blue dust and carefully apply to the remaining flowers and leaves **(C)**. Blend the second dust colour into the first by overdusting as desired.

**4.** Once you are happy with the effect, use a dry paintbrush to remove any excess dust from the stencil. This will prevent stray dust from falling as you lift it, spoiling the pattern beneath. Carefully lift the stencil away from the paste to reveal the pattern beneath **(D)**.

**5.** Carefully lift the stencilled paste from your work surface **(E)** and place it on another board or portable mat. This has a dual purpose: first, it will make lifting your cut-out tiles easier and secondly, it will declutter your work surface, enabling you to easily make a selection of different tiles.

**6.** Once transferred, use the largest cutter from the large Moroccan tile set to cut out a selection of tiles, positioning the cutter to make the pattern on each tile look attractive **(F)**. Cut as many tiles as you can before removing the excess paste.

**7.** Repeat Steps 1–6 using various stencils: six different stencil patterns were used on these tiles.

## WHITE-ON-DEEP BLUE TILES

**1.** Knead some deep blue modelling paste and roll it out on your work surface between 1mm (1⁄32in) spacers. Place the Chinese floral circle stencil on top of the paste and press down firmly with a smoother or rolling pin. If you use a rolling pin, make sure that the stencil doesn't move – this is especially important if you have to re-roll over it.

**2.** Using a finger or a suitable paintbrush, smear a thin layer of white vegetable fat (shortening) over the paste pattern showing through the stencil **(G)**.

**3.** Dip a large soft dusting brush into the edible lustre dust, knocking off any excess. Liberally dust over the stencil, adding more dust as necessary **(H)**, then use your brush to remove any excess dust from

## STENCIL STYLE

When choosing your stencils, make sure that the pattern detail is small enough to look attractive on the tiles.

## DUSTING KNOW-HOW

It is important to use the correct dusting brush to achieve a uniform appearance; if the bristles are too firm they may leave marks in the finish.

### HANDLE WITH CARE

Be very careful when handling the tiles as the dusts can smudge. Use a clean finger if you need to press the tile in place, and wash your hands in-between if you need to repeat this.

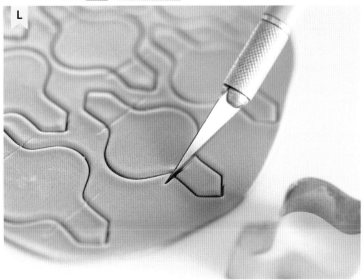

the stencil. Once all the excess is removed, use the brush to burnish the dust to make it really shine. Note: burnishing is not possible with all makes of dust food colour.

**4.** Carefully lift the stencil away from the paste to reveal the pattern. Lift the patterned paste, reposition it onto another board and then cut out the tiles (see Step 6, Blue-On-Deep Blue Tiles), choosing the positioning of the cutter carefully. Repeat Steps 1–4 using the cherry blossom stencil.

## ATTACHING THE TILES

### ADDING THE FIRST LAYER TO THE BASE TIER

**1.** While the tiles are still on their boards, select nineteen tiles in a mixture of patterns. Then take a craft knife and cut away the tops of these tiles, as shown **(I)**. Note: the remaining tiles will be used for the top tier.

**2.** Once the tiles are firm enough to be handled without distorting, carefully attach them individually around the top rim of the base tier using sugar glue, alternating the patterns and leaving a 1mm (1⁄32in) gap between each tile **(J)**.

**3.** Working around the cake, place a 1mm (1⁄32in) spacer between each tile to check the positioning **(K)**.

**4.** Roll out the deep blue paste, again between 1mm (1⁄32in) spacers. Cut out ten of the second tile shape from the largest Moroccan tile set. Take a craft knife and cut across each end of the tile, as shown **(L)**.

**5.** Leaving the two cut end sections on your work surface, remove all the excess paste and allow the shapes to firm up. Once they can be easily handled without distorting, attach them in the gaps between the tiles on the upper edge of the cake. Check that the tile pieces are positioned centrally in the spaces and, if necessary, cut away their tops so they sit flush against the top edge of the cake.

## ADDING THE FIRST LAYER TO THE TOP TIER

**1.** Using the medium tile set, first cut tiles from inside the leftover large tiles – there is no point in wasting these! Then create any more you may need. The top tier has over two rows of deep blue tiles: one of each shape, plus part of the small tile. Each row comprises 17 tiles.

**2.** Start by attaching the largest tiles in place with sugar glue, checking their vertical position with a set square and 1mm ($\frac{1}{32}$in) spacer. Next add the smaller tiles in a row above. To fill the gaps at the base of the top tier, cut the smaller shapes to size and attach in place.

## BRIGHT BLUE AND SKY BLUE TILES

Use the same method (see Making the Tiles) to create patterned tiles from both the bright blue and sky blue modelling pastes. You will need 19 tiles cut with the smaller rounded cutter from the large set for the base tier, and between 8 and 10 tiles cut with the larger, more pointed cutter from the medium set for the top tier. You will find that different stencils suit different cutters and that it is not just all-over patterned stencils that work; spot designs, such as the gem pendant shown here **(M)**, work really well, especially when used off-centre.

## BLUE-ON-WHITE TILES

Create these tiles following the same techniques (see Making the Tiles) using white modelling paste, three different stencils and the blue dusts. You will need approximately eight tiles cut with the largest cutter from the large set for the base tier and five tiles cut with the largest cutter from the medium set for the top tier. When using the mini check stencil, position the cutters so that the checks become diamonds, as shown **(N)**.

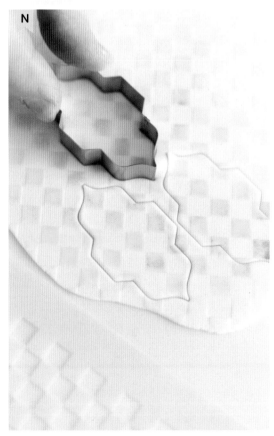

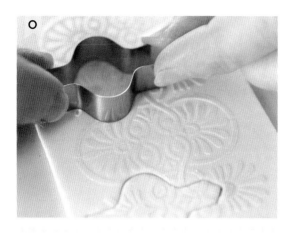

### WHITE-ON-WHITE TILES

**1.** Use a selection of suitable stencils, edible lustre dust and white modelling paste to create the white-on-white patterned tiles (see Making the Tiles). You will need about ten tiles using each cutter from the largest set, and three or four tiles using the largest cutter from the medium cutter set. The Greek repeat pattern stencil looks really attractive when cut out, as shown **(O)**.

### ADDING THE REMAINING TILES

**1.** Add the final top row of tiles to the top tier, mixing up the colours and patterns, as shown on the finished cake.

**2.** For the base tier, add a mixed row of bright blue and sky blue rounded tiles beneath the first deep blue row. Below this, add a row of predominantly white-on-white tiles, interspersed with a few blue-on-white tiles. Finally, add white-on-white rounded tiles in every other space below these.

## FINISHING TOUCHES

**1.** As this cake was covered in two sections, it is important to neaten the visible join at the top of the base tier. You will probably find that the sugarpaste around the join is not completely flat. To even this out, dilute some white sugarpaste by mixing cooled boiled water into it with a palette knife until it has a spreadable – but not sloppy – consistency. Use the palette knife to spread the icing over the join in the pastes, then smooth the icing and allow it to dry.

**2.** Knead the white modelling paste to warm it and roll it out between 1mm (1/32in) spacers into a long 60cm (23½in) strip. Accurately measure the distance between the top tier and the outer sugarpaste edge of the base tier and use a craft knife and straight edge to cut the strip to this width.

**3.** Position the modelling paste strip around the top of the base tier, cut away the excess and adjust to fit as necessary. Smooth the join closed.

### CUT TO PERFECTION

Don't be afraid to experiment – with some stencils, only part of the pattern will work well on the tile shapes.

**4.** Take the lace stick embosser and, positioning it up against the top tier, press down into the modelling paste strip, as shown **(P)**. (Note: the step photograph is shown on the finished cake, so just illustrates the position of the embosser.) Repeat until the embossed pattern encircles the top of the base tier. The embossing will alter the shape of the strip: trim it back as necessary with a craft knife.

**5.** Next roll out the deep blue modelling paste between the 1mm (⅛₂in) spacers into a 60cm (23½in) long strip. Using a straight edge and craft knife, cut a 2mm (¹⁄₁₆in) wide strip **(Q)**. Attach this to the top edge of the base cake for a neat finish.

## ADDING THE EDIBLE PAPER CARNATIONS

**1.** To add the carnations to the top of the base tier, first roll three balls of white sugarpaste, about 2cm (¾in) in diameter. Add a little piping gel to the back of each flower and press one into each sugarpaste ball. Attach the balls to the cake using sugar glue, as shown **(R)**.

**2.** At the wedding venue, place the cake on a cake stand and attach the remaining flowers in position, as shown on the finished cake.

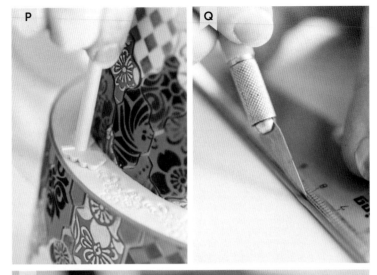

# Sensational Tiled Mini Cakes

These tiled mini cakes certainly have the wedding wow-factor! Start by baking and covering 5cm (2in) mini cakes with white sugarpaste. Now make a selection of tiles as for the main cake (see Making the Tiles) using Lindy's mini Moroccan tile set. Attach them around the base of each cake using sugar glue, and top each mini cake with a beautiful edible dahlia (see Edible Paper Flowers) in a complementary colour.

# RETRO CIRCLES

## SERVES 78

*The* circle theme of this rather special wedding cake is appropriately symbolic. Circles represent unity and wholeness and this cake has them in abundance: from the textured sphere of the top tier to the jewelled concentric rings of the middle tier, right down to the colourful rows of circles decorating the base. The use of traditional white as the main colour, with only small highlights of deep colour on the base tier, makes the two stylized red roses stand out for a fantastic focal point. The colours can be changed to suit any bridal colour scheme, but contrast is important here to make a real impact.

An array of techniques is used to create this striking three-tiered design. First, I embossed the board with a stencilled pattern and dusted it with lustre for extra sparkle. I decorated the base tier using a mixture of four circle patterns created in various colourways – you can easily alter the colours and patterns to suit the occasion. The tall middle tier looks elegant with its textured covering following the concentric pattern, and the addition of pearls, silver leaf and red edible flowers give the design a luxurious lift. Finally, I completely covered the top ball cake in white hundreds and thousands (nonpareils) to make a real statement.

## You will need

### CAKES

Bake, layer and stack your choice of cakes to create the following tier sizes:

★ **base tier:** 23cm (9in) round, 7.5cm (3in) deep

★ **second tier:** 17cm (6¾in) round, 16cm (6¼in) deep

★ **top tier:** 10cm (4in) ball

### MATERIALS

★ 3kg (6lb 8oz) white sugarpaste (rolled fondant)

★ white vegetable fat (shortening)

★ edible metallic white lustre dust (SK Snowflake)

★ **modelling paste:** 25g (1oz) each of 6 colours (see Colours); 250g (9oz) white

★ sugar glue

★ piping gel or confectioners' glaze (optional)

★ 2 sheets of silver leaf

★ white hundreds and thousands (nonpareils)

★ 5mm (¼in) pearlized ivory sugar pearls

★ **red edible wafer (rice) paper spiral flowers:** 1 large, 1 small (see Edible Paper Flowers)

### EQUIPMENT

★ **cake boards:** 30.5cm (12in) and 12.5cm (5in) round cake drums, round hardboards the same size as each cake

★ **dowels:** at least 18cm (7in) in length

★ **spacers:** 5mm (¼in); 1mm (¹⁄₃₂in)

★ palette knife

★ **stencils:** circle lattice – C778 (DS); Lindy's Greek repeat pattern – LC102 (LC)

★ smoother

★ soft dusting brush

★ 1m (40in) length of 1.5cm (⅝in) wide pink ribbon

★ non-toxic glue stick

★ set square

★ scriber

★ **piping tubes (tips):** nos. 18, 17, 2, 1.5 (PME)

★ craft knife

★ large textured raw silk rolling pin (HP)

★ multi-sized ribbon cutter (FMM)

★ greaseproof (wax paper)

★ pearl-headed dressmakers' pins

★ Dresden tool

★ **perfect pearl moulds:** 5mm (¼in); 4mm (⅛in); 3mm (¹⁄₁₆in) – BR130 (FI)

★ sugar shaper

★ selection of paintbrushes

### COLOURS

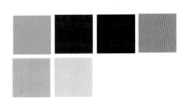

## Covering and assembling the cakes

**1.** Cover each of the cakes in turn with white sugarpaste (see Covering Cakes with Sugarpaste), remembering to place a hardboard cake board beneath each tier before covering. Use Method 3 to cover the base tier, covering the top first and then the sides. Cover the 12.5cm (5in) cake drum (the spacer beneath the ball cake) in the same way. Next, cover the second tier (the tall cake), using Method 5, again covering the top first followed by the sides. Finally, cover the ball cake (see Ball Cakes).

**2.** Dowel the base and second tier (see Dowelling Cakes).

## Covering the board

**1.** Cover the cake board with white sugarpaste (see Covering Boards) using 5mm (¼in) spacers. Use a palette knife to trim the soft sugarpaste to size and immediately position the circle lattice stencil on top of part of the covered board. Press a smoother firmly down on top of the stencil to force the sugarpaste to the upper surface of the stencil **(A)**. Reposition the smoother and repeat to emboss the entire stencil pattern into the soft sugarpaste.

**2.** Using a finger or suitable paintbrush, smear a thin layer of white vegetable fat over the surface of the sugarpaste pattern (the paste that has been forced up through the stencil).

**3.** Dip a soft dusting brush into the edible lustre dust and knock off any excess. Liberally dust over the stencil **(B)**, adding more dust as necessary. Use your brush to remove any excess: this will prevent stray dust falling from the stencil as you lift it, spoiling the pattern beneath. Once all the excess is removed, use the brush to burnish the dust for added shine. (Note: burnishing is not possible with all makes of dust food colour.)

### SOFTLY DOES IT

Use a soft brush for a uniform finish: if the bristles are too firm, they may leave marks in the finish.

**4.** Carefully peel the stencil away from the paste to reveal the pattern beneath **(C)**. Reposition the stencil, making sure the pattern aligns. Repeat the process twice more to completely cover the board.

**5.** Re-trim the board using a palette knife to give a neat finish. Secure the ribbon to the edge of the board using a non-toxic glue stick.

## Decorating the cakes

### BASE TIER

#### CIRCLE PATTERN ONE

**1.** Knead the pale pink modelling paste to warm it. Thinly roll out the paste between 1mm (⅟₃₂in) spacers to make a strip measuring at least 9cm (3½in) wide. Use a set square to accurately measure the height of your cake, then cut the rolled-out paste into a long rectangle of the same height. Ensure that all corners are square – accuracy is key here!

**2.** To make a placement guide, use the wider end of a PME piping tube (tip) to emboss a line of four evenly spaced circles along the short edge of your rectangle. This is a practise run! Repeat, adjusting the position of the circles as necessary – it may take a few attempts, so please be patient. Once you are happy with your spacing, cut out the line of circles and leave them on your work surface.

**3.** Using the embossed placement strip as a guide, lightly emboss three columns of circles onto the pale pink rectangle **(D)**. Using a set square and a craft knife, carefully cut out the block of embossed circles, ensuring that all edges are square **(E)**. Keep your placement guide for later.

C

### DUST GUARD

Once the sugarpaste is dry, spray the stencilled pattern with confectioners' glaze to set the dust and protect it from becoming smudged.

D

E

### PERFECT PASTE

Add a little white vegetable fat and water if your modelling paste is dry and crumbly – you need the paste to be pliable, but firm.

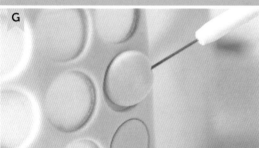

## EASY LIFTING

If your paste is distorting when you lift it, try adding a little more gum to it, or simply allow it to air dry for a few minutes before lifting.

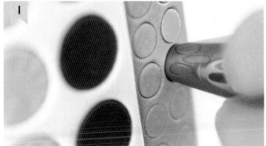

**4.** Attach the embossed paste to the side of your cake using a little water or sugar glue. Check the positioning of the paste, using a set square to make sure that the sides are vertical **(F)** and a smoother to check that the paste is flush with the top of the cake.

**5.** Use the wide end of the piping tube to cut through all the embossed circles (now on the cake) and remove each one with a scriber, as shown **(G)**.

**6.** Thinly roll out the green modelling paste between 1mm (¹⁄₃₂in) spacers. Place the Greek repeat pattern stencil on top of the paste and press down firmly with a smoother to force the modelling paste to the upper surface. Peel back the stencil to reveal the embossed pattern.

**7.** Use the wider end of a piping tube to cut out textured circles from the embossed pattern **(H)**. Insert the green textured circles into the middle column of the pale pink paste panel. Now cut additional circles from mid pink and purple modelling paste and attach these in place in the first and third columns.

## CIRCLE PATTERN TWO

**1.** Thinly roll out the mid pink modelling paste between 1mm (¹⁄₃₂in) spacers and cut it into a rectangle measuring the same height as your cake, ensuring that all corners are square.

**2.** Use a no. 18 piping tube to make a placement guide (see Step 2, Circle Pattern One). Once you are happy with your spacing, cut out the guide and leave it on your work surface. Use the guide to lightly emboss an additional two columns of small circles onto the mid pink rectangle. Cut to size and attach to the side of the cake using a little water or sugar glue. Check the positioning as before, then use the piping tube to cut out the columns of circles **(I)**. Remove each circle using a scriber and replace with red modelling paste circles, cut to the same size.

### CIRCLE PATTERN THREE

**1.** Roll out the light pink and purple modelling pastes between 1mm (¹⁄₃₂in) spacers and accurately cut into rectangles, measuring the height of the tier as before. Cut the width of the pale pink rectangle to approximately 2cm (¾in).

**2.** Cut the purple rectangle in two, then carefully lift and reposition the two purple rectangles, sandwiching the pale pink rectangle between them. Adjust the sides of the resulting rectangle, if necessary, with a set square and craft knife.

**3.** Using your first placement guide as a reference (see Step 2, Circle Pattern One), emboss two columns of circles centrally over the joins where the two colours meet **(J)**. Cut the rectangle to size and attach it to the side of the cake using a little water or sugar glue.

**4.** Cut out the circles as before, but this time replace them with vertical half circles of light pink and green, as shown **(K)**.

### CIRCLE PATTERN FOUR

Repeat Steps 1–7 of Circle Pattern One using a 2.2cm (⅞in) circle cutter to emboss and cut one column. Use the circle lattice stencil to add texture to the replacement circles **(L)**.

### COMPLETING THE TIER

Continue adding the four circle patterns until the sides of the cake are completely covered. Try varying the placement and colour of the patterns and the circle sizes.

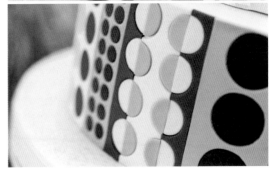

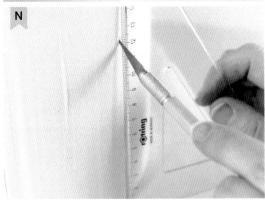

## CAREFUL MEASURING

Accuracy is key when cutting your paste: always ensure your pattern is vertical and all corners are square.

## SECOND TIER

### ADDING THE BACKGROUND

**1.** Using 1mm (¹⁄₃₂in) spacers, roll out a long strip of white modelling paste measuring at least 17cm (6¾in) wide. Take the large, textured raw silk rolling pin and firmly, but evenly, roll over the paste to add a fabric effect **(M)**.

**2.** Use a set square to accurately measure the height of your cake, then cut the textured paste into a long rectangle of the same height.

**3.** Paint sugar glue or cooled boiled water over the sides of your cake. Carefully pick up the textured paste and place it in position around the sides, ensuring that you don't stretch or distort the textured pattern while you do so.

**4.** Use a set square and craft knife to adjust the vertical sides of the paste strip as necessary **(N)**, then use a smoother to check the paste is flush with the top of the cake.

**5.** While the textured paste is still soft, take a large, soft dusting brush, dip it into the edible lustre dust and liberally dust all over the textured paste to add a shimmering finish **(O)**.

**6.** Add and dust other sections of textured paste until the sides of the cake are completely covered. The number of sections you need will depend upon the size of the rectangles you are adding. You may find it easier to apply smaller rectangles, in which case you will need to make more.

**7.** To make the vertical ribbons on the cake, thinly roll out some white modelling paste into 20cm (8in) long strips between the 1mm (1/32in) spacers. Using the multi-sized ribbon cutter on the 5mm (1/4in) setting, carefully but firmly roll the cutter through the paste in straight lines approximately 18 times **(P)**.

**8.** Attach the paste ribbons vertically to the side of the cake at random intervals, covering any joins in the textured paste. Cut to size with a craft knife, as shown **(Q)**.

### ADDING THE CIRCLE PATTERN

**1.** To make the circle template, cut out a piece of greaseproof (wax) paper to fit the front of your cake. Then draw three concentric circles onto the paper in the following sizes: 14cm (5½in), 8cm (3¼in) and 3cm (1⅛in).

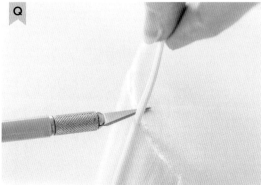

**2.** Temporarily secure the template to the cake using dressmakers' pins, aligning it so that the centre includes at least one of the paste ribbons. Prick dots all the way around each circle with a scriber **(R)**.

**3.** To make the strings of pearls, knead some white modelling paste to warm it and roll it into a long sausage shape, approximately 6mm (1/4in) thick. Place it on top of the 5mm (1/4in) section of the pearl mould and press the paste into the mould, first with your fingers, then using the back of a Dresden tool **(S)**. Use a palette knife to cut away the excess paste, then release the pearls by flexing the mould along its length to avoid breaking or distorting them **(T)**. Repeat using the 4mm (⅛in) and 3mm (1/16in) sections of the mould to create pearl strings in three different sizes.

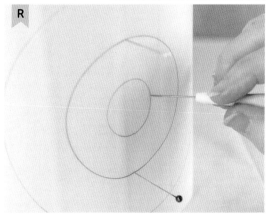

**4.** Use sugar glue to attach the pearl strings to the cake in vertical lines inside the outer two circles, as shown on the finished cake.

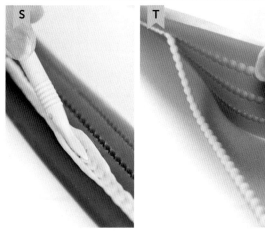

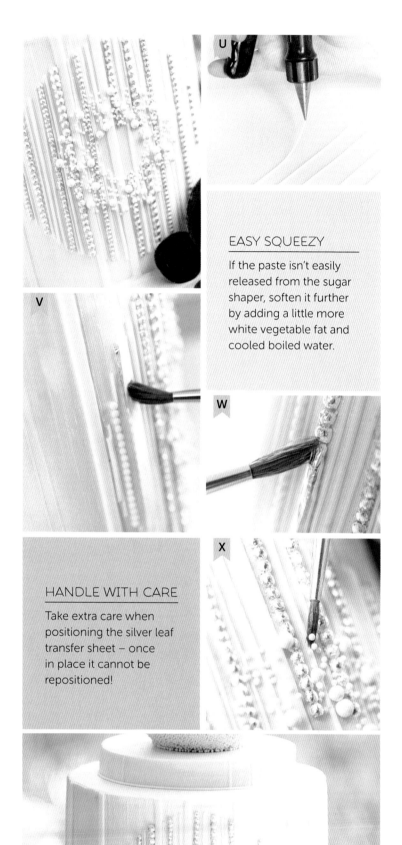

### EASY SQUEEZY

If the paste isn't easily released from the sugar shaper, soften it further by adding a little more white vegetable fat and cooled boiled water.

### HANDLE WITH CARE

Take extra care when positioning the silver leaf transfer sheet – once in place it cannot be repositioned!

**5.** Add a little white vegetable fat and cooled boiled water to some white modelling paste to make it really soft. Insert it inside the sugar shaper, together with the no. 1.5 piping tube. Push down the plunger and pump with the handle to squeeze out lengths of paste **(U)**. Insert the no. 2 piping tube into the sugar shaper and repeat. Allow the paste to firm up on your work surface, then cut it into lengths and attach it vertically inside the circle, referring to the finished cake for guidance.

**6.** To add the silver leaf, thinly brush the pearls with piping gel, sugar glue or confectioner's glaze and leave to dry until tacky. Cut a thin strip of silver leaf from the transfer sheet, position it accurately onto the cake and gently press onto the back of the transfer with a soft brush **(V)**. Leave in place for a moment then slowly peel away the backing paper. Very gently and carefully use a soft brush to push the silver leaf around the pearls **(W)**.

**7.** Finally, use sugar glue and a brush to add a random pattern of sugar pearls and white hundreds and thousands (nonpareils) to the middle circle **(X)**.

**8.** Make a large and small spiral flower (see Edible Paper Flowers) and set aside.

### THE SPACER

Cover the edges of the spacer with white modelling paste embossed with the large textured raw silk rolling pin, as for the second tier.

## THE BALL CAKE

**1.** Apply a coating of sugar glue to the covered ball cake and carefully tip white hundreds and thousands (nonpareils) over part of the glued area **(Y)**.

**2.** Once you have covered an area, use a paintbrush to remove most of the excess hundreds and thousands, then encourage the remaining to fill any gaps **(Z)**.

**3.** Continue until the whole of the cake is covered. You may find it easier to cover the underside of the ball first, or work in sections, allowing the glue to dry between each one.

## Assembling the cake

**1.** Using royal icing, attach the base tier centrally to the decorated board. Then attach the column cake to the top of the base tier, checking alignment and levels.

**2.** Attach the covered cake drum spacer to the centre of this tier. Finally, attach the ball cake onto the top of the spacer, checking alignment and levels.

**3.** Using the sugar shaper fitted with a no. 2 piping tube and softened white modelling paste, attach a squeezed-out length of paste around the base of the spacer, trimming it to fit with a craft knife.

**4.** Roll two balls of sugarpaste in appropriate sizes and attach them to the back of the edible paper flowers using piping gel. Experiment with placement and once you are happy, secure the flowers using sugar glue.

Y

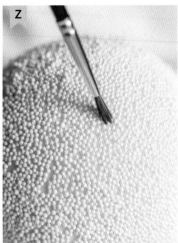

Z

## TIDY TIP

Place the ball cake on a plate or high-sided tray to catch any bouncing hundreds and thousands.

# Waistcoat and Bouquet Cookies

Using Lindy's bouquet and waistcoat cookie cutters (LC), bake and decorate the cookies using the same techniques and equipment as for the main cake. Decorate the bouquets with pearls, white hundreds and thousands (nonpareils) and spiral flowers created from 2.5cm (1in) circles (see Edible Paper Flowers). Form the stems by cutting into green sugarpaste with a palette knife then wrap them in white modelling paste, textured with a raw silk rolling pin.

To create the waistcoat, thinly roll out some white modelling paste, cut out a triangle for the shirt front and attach in place. Make two small pleats in thinly rolled-out red modelling paste, then cut out a diamond shape for the cravat and attach to the cookie. Add two thin strips and a ball of red paste for the knot. Roll out some white sugarpaste and emboss with the textured raw silk rolling pin. Cut out the waistcoat using the cookie cutter, remove a triangle of paste from the front and attach in place. Add the opening using a cutting wheel and the button detail with a piping tube. Finally, attach two small white triangles for the collar.

# SUMMERTIME BLOOMS

## SERVES 68

*This* beautiful, understated cake with its fresh citrus colours is wonderful for a summer wedding. Simple painted flowers printed onto floating fabrics originally inspired the charming design. The edible paper used to decorate the cake lends itself perfectly to replicate these soft, almost floating blooms, dappled in sunlight. With its overlapping floral decoration, striking highlights and subtle colouring, the central tier perfectly portrays a lush summer garden in bloom. A contemporary cake that can easily be adapted to any colour scheme, it will be the pièce-de-résistance at any outdoor reception venue.

The horizontal stripes in fresh springtime colours add a modern touch to this floral design. The stripes are cut from edible paper and painted with an oil-based paint, made by mixing food colour dust with vegetable oil. The overlapping blooms on the central tier were cut using either punches or a die cutter. I painted these with a range of brightly coloured oil-based paints, varying the intensity of the colours and adding contrasting details. An abundance of three-dimensional edible flowers in complementary shades completes the extravaganza.

## You will need

### CAKES

Bake, layer and stack your choice of cakes to create the following tier sizes:

★ **base tier:** 20cm (8in) round, 7.5cm (3in) deep

★ **second tier:** 15cm (6in) round, 19cm (7in) deep

★ **top tier:** 10cm (4in) round, 9cm (3½in) deep

### MATERIALS

★ 2.5kg (5lb 8oz) white sugarpaste (rolled fondant)

★ royal icing

★ 25g (1oz) white modelling paste

★ white vegetable fat (shortening)

★ sugar glue

★ white edible wafer (rice) paper

★ light vegetable oil, e.g. sunflower oil

★ **dust food colours:**
yellow (SK Sunflower); lime green (SK Vine); peach (SK Nasturtium); black (SK Blackberry); red (SK Poinsettia)

★ piping gel

★ **selection of edible wafer paper flowers:** Lindy used: 3 lime green carnations, 1 large and 2 medium orange chrysanthemums, 4 yellow dahlias and a few simple punched white daisies (see Edible Paper Flowers)

### EQUIPMENT

★ **cake boards:** 28cm (11in) round cake drum; 7.5cm (3in) board for the flower topper; round hardboards the same size as each cake

★ 90cm (35½in) length of 1.5cm (⅝in) wide green ribbon

★ non-toxic glue stick

★ **dowels:** at least 20cm (8in) in length

★ sugar shaper

★ no. 2 piping tube (tip) (PME)

★ craft knife

★ white paper

★ paintbrushes

★ greaseproof (wax) paper

★ pearl-headed dressmakers' pins

★ removable tape

★ die-cutting machine

★ **daisy flower punches:**
7.5cm (3in); 5cm (2in); 3.7cm (3½in); 2.5cm (1in); 1.7cm (⅝in)

★ **die templates:** 5.5cm (2¼in) classic scalloped circle; 2cm (¾in) flower centre (Xcut)

### COLOURS

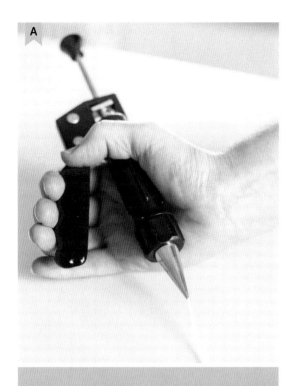

## SENSIBLE STACKING

When stacking your cake, use a level surface and a spirit level to ensure that each tier is perfectly horizontal and placed centrally before securing with royal icing.

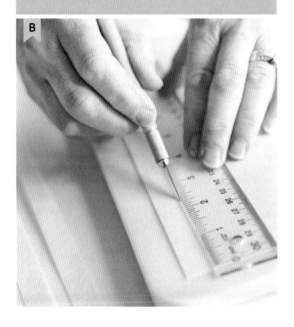

# Covering the cakes and board

**1.** Cover each of the cakes in turn as follows (see Covering Cakes with Sugarpaste), remembering to place a hardboard cake board beneath each tier before covering. Using white sugarpaste, cover the base and top tiers with Method 1 and cover the tall middle tier with Method 4. Finally, cover the cake drum (see Covering Boards) and allow to dry.

**2.** Use the non-toxic glue stick to attach the green ribbon around edge of the cake board.

**3.** Dowel the cakes, including the top tier (see Dowelling Cakes). Stack the cake, securing the tiers with royal icing.

# Decorating the cakes

## JOINING THE TIERS

**1.** To neaten the join between the base and first tier, first you will need to soften the white modelling paste. Add a little white vegetable fat (shortening) to the modelling paste to prevent it from becoming too sticky, then dunk it into a container of cooled boiled water, take it out and knead it. Repeat this process until the paste feels soft and stretchy.

**2.** Insert the softened paste into the barrel of the sugar shaper and add the no. 2 piping tube. Push down the plunger to remove any air, then pump the handle to squeeze out a 50cm (20in) length of paste onto your work surface **(A)**. Leave the paste to firm up for a few moments, then lift and attach around the join between the tiers using sugar glue to secure.

## ADDING HORIZONTAL STRIPS

**1.** Stack three sheets of white edible paper on top of each other on a suitable cutting surface. Using a ruler and craft knife, cut the following strips: three 1.5cm (⅝in) wide, three 1.1cm (½in) wide, three 8mm (⁵⁄₁₆in) wide and two 9mm (⅜in) wide **(B)**.

**2.** Place the three 1.5cm (⅝in) and two 9mm (⅜in) wide strips onto clean white paper. Mix a small amount of yellow dust food colour with a little vegetable oil to create an oil-based 'paint'.

**3.** Use the mixed oil-based paint to paint both sides of each strip **(C)**. You will find that the paint is readily absorbed into the textured side of the edible paper, but is not so easily applied into the smooth side. The distribution of colour may also be uneven, but don't worry, as it will even out a little as the paint dries – a slightly mottled appearance can also add more interest than a flat colour.

**4.** Transfer the painted strips, with their textured side uppermost, onto a fresh sheet of clean white paper and allow them to dry.

**5.** Paint the three 1.1cm (½in) strips lime green and the three 8mm (⁵⁄₁₆in) strips peach, mixing the dusts with oil as before. Then place them onto clean white paper and allow to dry.

**6.** Make two placement templates using greaseproof (wax) paper. Do this by measuring the circumference of your cake and then cutting two strips both slightly larger than this length: one 2.6cm (1in) wide and another 4.6cm (1¾in) wide.

**7.** Paint over the top surface of the three wider yellow painted strips with piping gel. Pick up a strip and position it around the bottom of the base cake, with the piping gel side facing the cake to act as a glue. Press on the strip to make sure it is well secured, adding more piping gel to the ends if necessary. The paper will initially have a tendency to curl away from the cake, but don't panic: it can easily be encouraged to stay in place with the temporary help of dressmakers' pins. Pick up the next strip and position it, abutting one end against the first strip. Add the final strip, pin in place and cut to size with scissors.

**8.** Once the strips are securely in place, remove any pins. Then wrap the 2.6cm (1in) wide placement template around the base of the cake and temporarily secure in place with removable tape. Next paint piping gel over the painted green strips and attach in place with pins above the template, cutting away the excess from the third strip using scissors **(D)**. Repeat for the orange strips using the 4.6cm (1¾in) wide template.

**9.** Add the two remaining 9mm (³⁄₈in) yellow strips around the base of the top tier, again using piping gel and cutting to size as before.

## HAND PAINT WITH OIL PAINT

Water-based paints don't work when hand painting on edible paper, as they rapidly dissolve the paper.

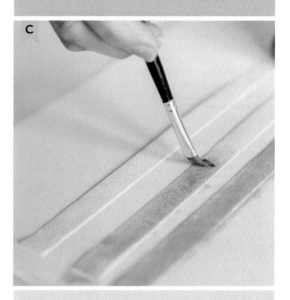

## UNIFORM COLOURS

If the colours where the strips join are notably different, simply touch them up with a little more of the edible oil paint.

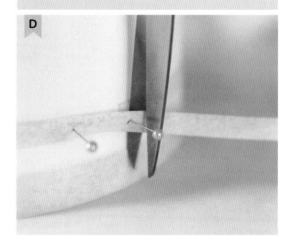

## PLAN AHEAD

These painted flowers can easily be created in advance and stored in plastic bags or boxes until needed.

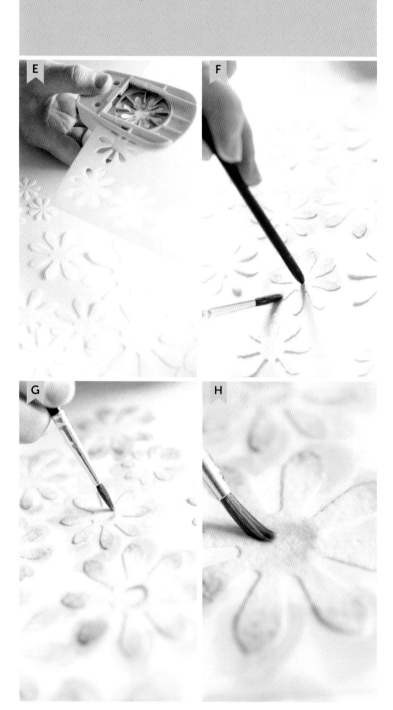

## CREATING THE PAINTED FLOWERS

### THE GREEN FLOWERS

**1.** Slide the back off one of the punches, then keeping this punch upside down, slide in up to four stacked sheets of white edible paper. Experiment to see how many flowers you can cleanly cut at once – this will depend on the sharpness of the cutting edges.

**2.** Firmly squeeze the handle closed to punch out a flower from each sheet of paper.

**3.** Carefully remove the punch, taking care not to get any paper stuck in the punch itself. Reposition the punch as close as you can to the first flower to avoid wasting paper and punch out as before **(E)**. Continue until you have a selection of flowers in each different size.

**4.** Place the edible paper flowers with their rough side uppermost on a sheet of clean white paper. Load the brush with clear oil, dip it into the mixed green paint made for the strips and paint each petal **(F)**. By loading the brush in this way, you can easily create petals with varying intensities of colour.

**5.** Using a small, clean brush and the yellow paint used for the strips, paint small 'C' shapes in the centre of each flower **(G)**. Use the end of a paintbrush to hold the flowers still while you paint. Take another clean brush, dip it into the clear oil and paint over the centre of each flower **(H)**. The addition of the oil spreads the yellow paint to give it a more subtle appearance.

**6.** Mix up some edible black dust with oil and use to paint around the centre of each flower **(I)**.

**7.** Transfer the painted flowers onto a fresh sheet of white paper and allow to dry. Once dry, place one painted flower on top of another of the same size and secure together using a tiny amount of piping gel **(J)**.

## THE RED FLOWERS

Using the three smallest punches and red dust food colour mixed with oil, create the flowers in the same way as in the photographs (see The Green Flowers).

## THE YELLOW FLOWERS

**1.** Punch out a selection of edible paper flowers and paint the petals yellow, as before. Paint clear oil over the centre of each flower. Mix up some red paint using dust food colour and oil, then stipple over parts of the centre of each flower **(K)**.

**2.** Dip a fine paintbrush into the black paint and add a few random dots to add interest. Finally, add touches of green **(L)** and red paint to the edges of some of the flower petals.

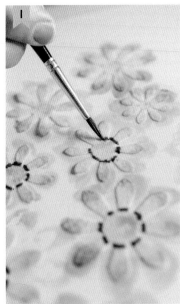

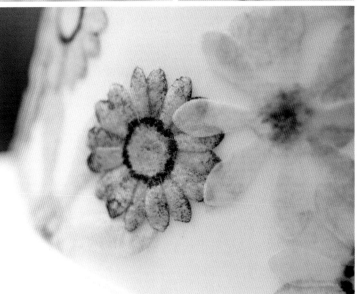

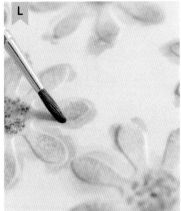

## USEFUL TOOL

Dies and die-cutting machines are easier to store and much more economical in the long run than buying lots of punches. If you don't have one, see if you can borrow a machine to try it out.

## THE RED SCALLOPED CIRCLE FLOWER

**1.** The intricate scalloped circles on this flower are cut using a die-cutting machine. Cut sheets of edible paper to fit through the die cutter and set up the base plates with the edible paper, the classic scallop circle die and the flower centre die, following the manufacturer's instructions. Turn the handle to cut out the shapes (I cut four shapes at once), then reposition the die and repeat **(M)**. You will need five or six of each shape. If your centres don't pop out easily, use the tip of a craft knife or scriber to release them.

**2.** Place the scalloped circles and flower centres on a sheet of clean white paper, with their rough side uppermost. Paint the outer edges of each scalloped circle with red paint and the middle of each central part with yellow paint **(N)**. Use a clean brush to paint over the flower with clear oil – this will allow the colours to defuse and mix.

**3.** Paint each of the flower centres black and add one to each flower, using a brush to aid placement **(O)**.

## ADDING THE FLOWERS TO THE CAKE

**1.** Once dry, position the flowers on the cake with pearl-headed pins. Experiment with placement and overlap some of the flowers, starting with the larger flowers and filling in with the smaller ones **(P)**. Where a flower meets the base tier, simply use scissors to make a straight cut across a section of the flower, so that it fits snugly.

**2.** Start by sticking the flowers that make up the background in place – those that will have other flowers overlapping them. Move the flower up the pin towards the pearl pinhead, then take a damp paintbrush and slightly wet the back of each petal **(Q)**. Push the flower back down the pin onto the surface of the cake and use a dry paintbrush to carefully press the petals in place **(R)**. Once the flower is secure, remove the pin. Continue until all flowers are securely attached and all pins are removed.

**3.** If desired, touch up any sections of the flowers that you would like to brighten up or enhance. For example, the definition of some of my black circles had disappeared and needed a little extra paint **(S)**.

## THE FLORAL TOPPER

**1.** Cover the 7.5cm (3in) hardboard cake board with a shallow dome of white sugarpaste and attach it to the top of your stacked cake using royal icing (see Covering Boards).

**2.** Using piping gel as a glue, stick your prepared selection of edible wafer paper flowers around and over the dome, using the photos as a reference.

### ON OR OFF

I prefer to glue the flowers in position on the cake, but you might find it easier to remove each flower from the cake before wetting the back with a damp paintbrush.

# Champagne Party Cookies

The perfect addition to a wedding reception or hen party. Use Lindy's fitted dress cookie cutter (LC) to bake the floral dress cookies, then simply cover with white sugarpaste and add the flowers as for the main cake.

Bake the champagne glass cookies using Lindy's champagne glass cookie cutter (LC). Separately roll out some white and cream sugarpaste and cut out a glass shape from each colour for all the cookies. Using a craft knife, cut a curve separating the stem from the top of each glass. Attach a white stem and cream top to each cookie with piping gel and smooth the stems with your fingers to round the cut edges. Cut bubbles from thinly rolled white modelling paste using small round piping tubes and gently press them into the soft cream sugarpaste.

# FLAMBOYANT FLEUR-DE-LIS

## SERVES 122

*This* large, impressive masterpiece has a more macho feel to it than a traditional wedding cake. Lace and flowers are not everyone's idea of a dream design, and here the stylized flower shape of the fleur-de-lis is teamed up with powerful chevrons to create the perfect alternative: a distinctive statement wedding cake in strong, contrasting colours. The fleur-de-lis motif is an ancient symbol that can trace its roots back as far back as Mesopotamia. It is, however, still very much in use today and is said to symbolize perfection, light and life, making it ideal as a wedding motif.

*J*nnovative silicone onlays gave me the inspiration for this eye-catching design, which showcases the elegant fleur-de-lis motif. I used black modelling paste and a fleur-de-lis onlay to decorate the base tier and a savvy chevron onlay with brightly coloured paste to embellish the second. A pasta machine was useful for ensuring my modelling paste was rolled out to an even thickness. The statement fleur-de-lis on the third tier was cut using my large fleur-de-lis motif cutter set, and the beautiful beading on the top tier was simply made using a perfect pearl mould. Each pearl was dusted with edible gold lustre dust for a glistening effect.

# *You will need*

## CAKES

Bake, layer and stack your choice of cakes to create the following tier sizes:

★ **base tier:** 25.5cm (10in) round, 10cm (4in) deep

★ **second tier:** 20cm (8in) round, 8.5cm (3⅜in) deep

★ **third tier:** 15cm (6in) round, 18.5cm (7¼in) deep

★ **fourth tier:** 9cm (3½in) round, 2.5cm (1in) deep

★ **top tier:** 6.5cm (2½in) round, 6.5cm (2½in) deep

## MATERIALS

★ **sugarpaste (rolled fondant):** 1.5kg (3lb 5oz) white; 2kg (4lb 8oz) gold; 1kg (2lb 4oz) deep orange; 250g (9oz) black

★ light gold edible lustre dust (SK)

★ cornflour (cornstarch) for dusting

★ **modelling paste:** 200g (7oz) black; 100g (3½oz) deep orange; 50g (1¾oz) peach; 50g (1¾oz) white; 150g (5½oz) gold

★ sugar glue

★ white vegetable fat (shortening)

★ royal icing

## EQUIPMENT

★ **cake boards:** 33cm (13in) round cake drum; round hardboards the same size as each cake

★ **brushes:** large soft-bristled brush, small paintbrush

★ **dowels:** at least 20cm (8in) in length

★ dusting bag or small square of muslin

★ pasta machine (optional)

★ **Silicone Onlays®:** fleur-de-lis, savvy chevron (MM)

★ scriber

★ **spacers:** 5mm (¼in); 2mm (1⁄16in); 1mm (1⁄32in)

★ **cutters:** Lindy's pointed oval set (LC); Lindy's large fleur-de-lis motif cutter set (LC); Lindy's curled leaf set (LC); Lindy's Indian scroll set (LC); no. 6 frill cutter (FMM)

★ piping (pastry) bag

★ piping tubes (tips): nos. 17, 2, 1.5, 1 (PME)

★ craft knife

★ rolling pin

★ greaseproof (wax) or tracing paper

★ pearl-headed dressmakers' pins

★ **perfect pearl moulds:** 5mm (¼in); 6mm (¼in); 8mm (5⁄16in); 10mm (⅜in) – BR130 and BR129 (FI)

★ vintage brooch mould (KD)

★ ball tool

★ sugar shaper

★ Dresden tool

★ 105cm (41⅜in) length of 1.5cm (⅜in) wide gold ribbon and braid

★ non-toxic glue stick

## COLOURS

# Covering the cakes and board

**1.** Cover each of the cakes in turn as follows (see Covering Cakes with Sugarpaste), remembering to place a hardboard cake board beneath each tier before covering. Use Method 2 to cover the base tier with white sugarpaste, keeping its top edge as sharp as possible.

**2.** Cover the second tier and fourth tier with gold-coloured sugarpaste using Method 1. Cover the cake drum with the remaining gold-coloured sugarpaste (see Covering Boards). Then use a large soft-bristled brush to liberally dust the gold edible lustre dust over the surface of the fresh gold-coloured sugarpaste.

**3.** Use Method 5 to cover the third tier with deep orange sugarpaste, covering the top first followed by the sides.

**4.** Finally, cover the top tier with black sugarpaste using Method 1.

**5.** Dowel all the cakes except the top tier (see Dowelling Cakes).

# Decorating the cakes

## THE BASE TIER

**1.** Using a dusting bag, dust the fleur-de-lis silicone onlay with cornflour (cornstarch) **(A)**. Shake off the excess to leave only a very fine covering over the surface of the onlay.

**2.** Set up your pasta machine and experiment with the width settings using small pieces of modelling paste (I set the rollers to number five on my machine, but yours may differ); you will need to roll out paste that is fractionally thinner than the depth of the cutting edges on the silicone onlay.

**3.** Knead some of the black modelling paste to warm it, then roughly roll it out into a 10cm (4in) wide strip. Feed it through your pasta machine on the appropriate setting **(B)**. If you don't have a pasta machine, you can roll the paste by hand, although it can be quite difficult.

**4.** Place the thinned modelling paste over the fleur-de-lis onlay and dust over the top surface of the paste with cornflour **(C)**. Using your fingers, a rolling pin or a combination of the two, press the paste into the onlay so that the cutting edges cleanly cut through it **(D)**. It can take a little patience and practise to use the onlays at first, but you'll soon get the hang of them!

**5.** Use a scriber to remove the unwanted sections of paste **(E)**. Paint over the remaining patterned pieces with sugar glue and leave the glue to go tacky **(F)**.

**6.** Pick up the onlay and stretch it gently in various directions to loosen the paste pieces, ensuring that they will be easily released. Place the onlay in position on the side of the cake and rub over the back with your hands to help the paste adhere to the cake. Carefully peel the onlay away to reveal the fleur-de-lis pattern beneath **(G)**. If necessary, use a dry paintbrush to fractionally adjust the position of the paste pieces.

**7.** Repeat using the onlay's integral placement guides until the pattern completely encircles the cake.

**8.** Roll out some white modelling paste between the 1mm (1⁄32in) spacers. Use the 2.7cm (1⅛in) pointed oval cutter to cut out one oval for each large fleur-de-lis. Attach, using sugar glue and a paintbrush **(H)**. The paintbrush is used to help position the shapes, as well as to spread the glue.

### PERFECT FIT

You may need to adjust the last pattern to make it fit neatly.

### USE YOUR FINGERS

While the rolling pin helps to secure the peach paste inside the onlay, if you roll over the lower section there is a danger that the peach paste will become attached to the deep orange!

**9.** Brush each black fleur-de-lis with white vegetable fat (shortening). This will add shine, remove any cornflour residue and help to prevent the black icing from bleeding into the piped royal icing dots – particularly important if the cake is to be kept for any length of time.

**10.** Fill a piping (pastry) bag fitted with a coupler and no. 1.5 piping tube (tip) with freshly paddled royal icing. The consistency of your icing is critical here; you want to be able to quickly and easily pipe rounded dots, rather than pointed cones. Starting on the outside of the top of the large fleur-de-lis, hold the tip fractionally away from the side of the cake and squeeze the bag until you have a dot of icing of the required size. Release the pressure and only then remove the tip – squeeze, release and remove. Leave a small gap and pipe the next dot, then continue to pipe dots around the top and bottom sections of all the large fleur-de-lis. Add a piped dot to the top and bottom tip of each white pointed oval.

**11.** Change the tube in the coupler to a no. 1 and pipe dots around sections of the small vertical fleur-de-lis and the sides of the white ovals **(I)**.

**12.** Using a craft knife and thinly rolled-out black modelling paste, cut 8mm ($\frac{5}{16}$in) and 4mm ($\frac{1}{8}$in) squares. Add one of each to the white oval section on each large fleur-de-lis, as shown.

## THE SECOND TIER

**1.** This tier is decorated using the savvy chevron onlay. The process is almost the same as for the base tier, however this time two colours and only three-quarters of the pattern are used. First prepare the onlay and paste as before (see Base Tier, Steps 1–4) and create the first layer from the deep orange modelling paste.

**2.** For the second row of chevrons, place the prepared peach-coloured modelling paste in position and roll over the top half of the pattern with a rolling pin, taking care not to roll over the deep orange chevrons **(J)**. Use your fingers to rub over the lower part of the chevron to obtain a clean cut. Carefully peel away all the unwanted sections of paste **(K)**.

**3.** Create the third row of chevrons from the deep orange paste and attach the completed pattern to the cake as before (see Base Tier, Steps 5–6). Repeat, using the onlay's integral placement guides, until the pattern completely encircles the cake. Adjust the last pattern, if necessary, so that it fits neatly.

**4.** To make the white pattern details, start by thinly rolling out a little white modelling paste. Using the no. 17 piping tube as a circle cutter, cut out and attach a circle just above the central 'V' of each of the bottom row of chevrons. Pipe dots of white royal icing in the centre of each circle using a no. 2 piping tube, then change to a no. 1 piping tube to add dots above and below, as shown.

## THE THIRD TIER

**1.** Make a fleur-de-lis template by drawing around each piece of the fleur-de-lis cutter set with a pencil onto greaseproof or tracing paper **(L)**. The crown and large leaf shape are used once, whereas the other four shapes are repeated, mostly as mirror images.

**2.** Secure the template to the cake with dressmakers' pins. Use a scriber to prick out the outline to help with placement **(M)**. Remove the template and set aside – this will be used to construct the fleur-de-lis.

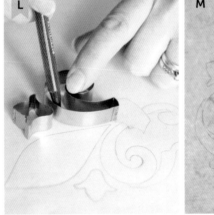

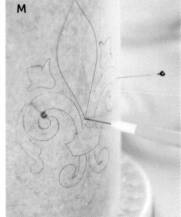

### CAREFUL PLACEMENT

For neat results, make sure that the overall shape is symmetrical when drawing the fleur-de-lis design, and secure it centrally onto the cake.

**3.** Roll out some black sugarpaste between the 5mm (¼in) spacers and cut out all the shapes except the crown and outer flourishes **(N)**. Use a finger to smooth the cut edges of each shape for a softer, more rounded appearance **(O)**.

**4.** Once each shape is ready, position them onto the template created in Step 1 **(P)**. Use the same method to cut out the crown from 5mm (¼in) thick gold sugarpaste and the flourishes from 2mm (¹⁄₁₆in) thick black modelling paste.

**5.** Roll out some white modelling paste between 1mm (¹⁄₃₂in) spacers and cut out one 5.5cm (2¼in) pointed oval, two curled leaves, two Indian scrolls and one small circle using the no. 17 piping tube, as shown **(Q)**. Attach these in place, referring to the finished cake for guidance.

**6.** Roll graduated balls of gold modelling paste and place these on the points of the crown. Using the 5mm (¼in) perfect pearl mould, make a short string of gold pearls and use sugar glue to attach them to the crown in an upward curve **(R)**.

**7.** To create the brooch above the crown, knead a small amount of white modelling paste and roll it into a ball, smaller than the centre of the round brooch in the vintage brooch mould. Press the ball into the centre of the mould using a ball tool **(S)**.

**8.** Roll a ball of black modelling paste slightly larger than the mould cavity and position it into the mould, ensuring that the sugar surface being placed into the mould is perfectly smooth. Firmly push the paste into the mould and remove the excess paste with a palette knife, so the back of the mould is flat. Carefully flex the mould to release the paste **(T)**.

**9.** Create two square studs using the same mould and black modelling paste.

**10.** Use sugar glue to attach all the prepared elements to the cake, using the placement lines or points as a guide.

**11.** Add a little white vegetable fat (shortening) and cooled boiled water to soften some of the black modelling paste. Place it, together with the small round disc, inside the sugar shaper and push down the plunger and pump, using the handle to squeeze out two lengths of paste **(U)**. Allow the paste to firm up on your work surface, cut into approximately 4cm (1½in) lengths and attach to the fleur-de-lis to help join up all the elements.

### LESS IS MORE

Use just enough white modelling paste to line the centre section. This will prevent it from spreading into the surrounding area when the black paste is added.

### SOFTLY DOES IT

You need to use modelling paste that is really quite soft in the sugar shaper, otherwise it won't come out easily.

**12.** To finish the fleur-de-lis, mix gold lustre dust with water and paint over the crown and its embellishments to gild them. Brush the black areas with white vegetable fat to add a shine and help prevent the black colour from bleeding into the piped royal icing dots. Use royal icing and the various sized piping tubes to pipe royal iced dots on elements of the design, as shown.

## THE FOURTH TIER

**1.** To create the gold beading, knead some gold modelling paste to warm it, then roll it into a long sausage, approximately 1cm (⅜in) thick. Place it on top of the 8mm (⁵⁄₁₆in) section of the perfect pearl mould and press the paste into the mould, first with your fingers then using the back of a Dresden tool **(V)**. Use a palette knife to cut away the excess paste, then release the pearls by flexing the mould along its length, so the pearls fall out without breaking or distorting **(W)**. Repeat to make enough pearls to wrap around the tier four times.

**2.** Allow the pearls to firm up a little, then attach in position on the cake using sugar glue. Once complete, dust over the pearls with edible gold lustre dust until they glisten **(X)**.

### USEFUL TOOL

Use a smoother to help roll out the sausages of gold paste, applying just enough pressure so the paste lengthens evenly as you roll.

## Assembling the cake

**1.** Using royal icing to secure, stack the cakes onto the cake board, checking alignment and levels as you go and referring to the finished cake for reference.

**2.** Create strings of pearls using the 6mm (¼in) pearl mould and gold modelling paste. Dust each string with gold lustre dust, and then use sugar glue to attach the strings around the base of the stacked cake.

**3.** Using white royal icing and a no. 2 piping tube, pipe a row of small, evenly spaced dots over the join between the first and second tiers.

**4.** To create the trim around the base of the third tier, thinly roll out some gold modelling paste between 1mm (¹⁄₃₂in) spacers. Take the no. 6 frill cutter and firmly press it into the paste. Take a straight edge and craft knife and cut along the paste to create a neat edging **(Y)**. Cut another two, then brush edible gold lustre dust over the trim **(Z)**. Remove any excess dust and attach the trim around the base of the cake, using sugar glue to secure it in place.

**5.** Roll out the deep orange modelling paste to 1mm (¹⁄₃₂in) using spacers. Cut a 1cm (³⁄₈in) wide ribbon and attach it around the top outer edge of the third tier to disguise the join in the paste.

**6.** Use the non-toxic glue stick to secure the ribbon and braid to the edge of the cake board.

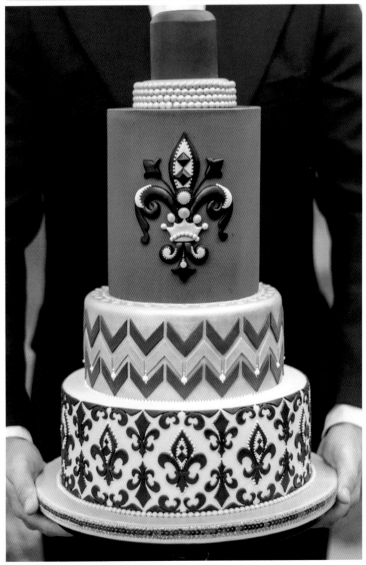

# Fleur-de-lis Cupcakes

These dazzling cupcakes are the perfect accompaniment to the tiered cake. Bake the cupcakes in black cases (liners) and cover with deep orange, gold and white sugarpaste. Decorate with statement fleur-de-lis motifs, simply cut from black modelling paste using the fleur-de-lis onlay. Royal-iced piped details add a special finishing touch.

# DESIGNER DOODLE ART

## SERVES 55

For many people, doodling is something that is done absent-mindedly; patterns are scribbled on pads of paper when talking on the phone, or hand drawn onto napkins while waiting in a café. However, doodling or 'tangling' has recently been promoted as a therapeutic art form where each design is executed slightly differently, but all are essentially hand drawn with repetitive patterns. Doodle patterns embellish the symmetrical flower shapes on this essentially floral wedding cake, which is very relaxing and rewarding to create. There is a lot of scope to really personalize this design, simply by including shapes and motifs that are special to the wedding couple.

*I* thoroughly enjoyed doodling a variety of patterns onto this cake, from straight lines and scrolls to arcs and borders. I highly recommend the Kemper fluid writer tool, which will enable you to effortlessly draw patterns onto your cake. The flowers embellishing the lower tiers are cut from modelling paste using a variety of cutters, which are carefully layered for a three-dimensional look. The statement monogram can be created using your computer to make it truly personal. I traced my monogram onto the cake, painted it with sugar glue, used a sugar shaper to squeeze lengths of paste over the design and then highlighted areas with the fluid writer. The final flourish is the edible paper bow, which finishes the design perfectly.

## You will need

### CAKES

Bake, layer and stack your choice of cakes to create the following tier sizes:

★ **base tier:** 20cm (8in) round, 7.5cm (3in) deep

★ **second tier:** 15cm (6in) round, 12cm (4¾in) deep

★ **top tier:** 10cm (4in) round, 9cm (3½in) deep

### MATERIALS

★ **sugarpaste (rolled fondant):** 1.6kg (3lb 8oz) white; 150g (5½oz) pink

★ royal icing

★ piping gel

★ **modelling paste:** 120g (4¼oz) white; 50g (1¾oz) dark pink; 25g (1oz) mid pink; 50g (1¾oz) pale pink; 25g (1oz) very pale pink; 15g (½oz) black

★ sugar glue

★ black liquid food colour (SK)

★ pink edible wafer (rice) paper

★ white vegetable fat (shortening)

★ pink hybrid musk rose (see Edible Paper Flowers)

### EQUIPMENT

★ **cake boards:** 28cm (11in) round cake drum; round hardboards the same size as each cake and the spacer

★ round polystyrene spacer 10cm (4in) round, 2cm (¾in) deep

★ Baking (parchment) paper, greaseproof (wax) paper

★ pins or removable tape

★ scriber

★ 1mm (¹⁄₃₂in) spacers

★ **selection of flower cutters:** Lindy used: daisy marguerite plunger cutters – set of 4 (PME); 5 petal cutters – set of 4 (PME); Lindy's flat floral collection – set 1 and 2 (LC); single rose cutter (FMM); veined large sunflower cutter (PME); veined sunflower; gerbera and daisy cutters – set of 3 (PME); carnation cutter set (FMM); 9.5cm (3¾in) scalloped circle pastry cutter; wavy circle cutter set

★ rolling pin

★ palette knife

★ craft knife

★ small fluid writer (KT)

★ paintbrush or eyedropper

★ kitchen paper (paper towel)

★ white paper

★ paintbrush

★ pencil

★ pearl-headed dressmakers pins

★ no. 1.5 piping tube (tip) (PME)

★ sugar shaper

★ **dowels:** at least 16cm (6¼in) in length

★ set square

★ 90cm (35½in) length of 1.5cm (⅝in) wide pink ribbon

★ non-toxic glue stick

### COLOURS

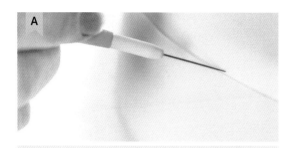

A

### EVENLY SPACED

It is important to use spacers when rolling out the modelling paste to ensure that all your flowers are the same thickness.

B

C

## Covering the cakes and board

**1.** Using white sugarpaste, cover the board (see Covering Boards) and cakes using Method 1 (see Covering Cakes with Sugarpaste) and place to one side. Remember to place a hardboard cake board beneath each tier before covering.

**2.** Attach the polystyrene spacer to its hardboard cake board using royal icing. Once set, cover the sides of the separator with piping gel. Roll out the pink sugarpaste and cut it into a 32 × 2.3cm (12½ × ⅞in) strip. Attach the strip around the sides of the separator and place to one side to dry.

## Decorating the cakes

### PREPARING THE BASE TIER

Measure the circumference of your cake. Cut a strip slightly larger than this length x 6.5cm (2½in) wide from baking or greaseproof paper. Temporarily secure the strip around the base tier using pins or removable tape, then use a scriber to score all the way around the top edge **(A)**. This will ensure that when you are doodling, the top edge of the pattern remains neat and horizontal.

### THE FLOWERS

#### CUTTING OUT THE FLOWERS

**1.** Separately knead the different modelling paste colours until they are warm and stretchy, then roll out each colour on your work surface between 1mm (¹⁄₃₂in) spacers.

**2.** Cut out flowers from these rolled-out pastes using the suggested flower cutters, as shown **(B)**. To use many of the cutters, simply press the cutter into the rolled-out paste and give it a little wiggle before removing the cutter and excess paste.

**3.** To use the plunger cutters, press your chosen plunger into the rolled-out modelling paste and wiggle the cutter quickly from side to side. The paste should come up with the cutter as you lift it. Rub your finger or the pad of your thumb over the cutter to remove any small flecks of paste **(C)**. Finally, press down on the plunger to release the shape back onto your work surface.

**4.** To use the more intricate cutters, place the rolled-out paste over the cutter – rather than pressing the cutter into the paste – and roll over with a rolling pin **(D)**. Rub your finger over the edges of the cutter to help cut through the thickness of the paste, then turn the cutter over and carefully press out the paste using a soft paintbrush.

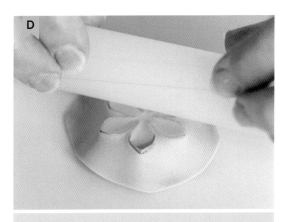

**5.** Once you have cut out your flowers, leave them to firm up for a moment or two, to help prevent the shapes distorting. Loosen the flowers from your work surface by slicing a palette knife underneath.

### ATTACHING THE FLOWERS TO THE CAKES

**1.** Selecting your cut-out shapes carefully, stack one on top of another **(E)**. You don't need to stack all the shapes; the number of layers is up to you (I used a maximum of three layers). Remember to leave room for embellishing the petals later.

**2.** Start attaching the flowers around the base tier with sugar glue **(F)**, leaving wide gaps for doodling in-between each flower.

**3.** Where a flower crosses over the scribed line, cut along this line with a craft knife **(G)** and remove any petal sections from above the line. Where a flower is to be positioned at the base of the cake, cut a straight line across part of it while it is on your work surface, before you add it to the cake.

**4.** When adding flowers to the second tier, attach the large central white flower first. Next add flowers around it and to the lower edge of the rest of the cake.

## THE DOODLING

**1.** To doodle onto a covered cake effortlessly, enjoyably and successfully, you will need to invest in the correct tool; you could use an edible food pen, but after a while you will struggle! The tool you will require is a Kemper fluid writer: a precision engineered tool that holds like a brush, writes like a pen, can be easily used on vertical surfaces and doesn't drip. Use a paintbrush or eyedropper to fill the cup of the fluid writer with black liquid food colour.

### SMOOTH EDGES

If the edges of your shape become feathered, as can happen with some cutters, carefully press the feathering underneath with a finger.

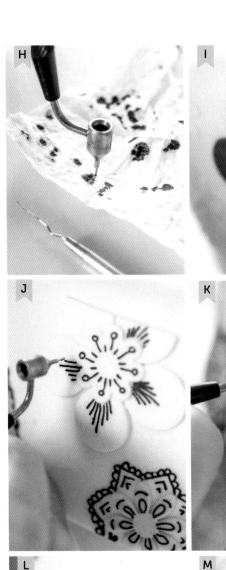

**2.** Holding the tool like a paintbrush, lightly touch the tip to the flower surface where you wish to start, As soon as you make contact with the paste, the liquid food colour will be released. Let the tip glide over the flower to create a pattern and remove the tip when you wish to stop. Never press down on the tip: it needs to simply glide over the surface. If the tip gets blocked, for example if you accidentally push it into your icing, push the thin metal wire provided with the fluid writer through the cup and out of the bottom of the tip to release it. Use kitchen paper to encourage the food colour to flow freely before you begin a section **(H)**.

**3.** You can use many different patterns to doodle onto your cake. Here are some ideas:

**Scrolls:** Starting at the centre, draw a scroll large enough to fill each petal **(I)**.

**Straight lines:** Lines of varying lengths are easy to apply and can look really effective **(J)**.

**Dots:** To make small dots, quickly touch the surface with the tip of the fluid writer and remove it **(K)**. For larger dots, leave the tip in one place to allow the food colour to pool.

**Arcs:** Curved lines are drawn from one area to another to enlarge the size of the flowers beyond their cut-out shapes **(L)**.

**Border patterns:** There are many ways to add these; here the arcs are simply divided up by adding lines to make small rectangles **(M)**.

**4.** Doodle over and around each flower, using the close-up photographs for inspiration. Remember, it doesn't matter if your hand slips or the flowers become lopsided: this only adds to the charm of the design.

**5.** To fill in some of the areas between the flowers, either draw cross-hatched lines and infill every other square **(N)** or draw bubbles of varying sizes to fill the gaps **(O)**.

## PRACTISE MAKES PERFECT

To gain confidence with your doodling, practise on a few spare flowers first before starting on the cake.

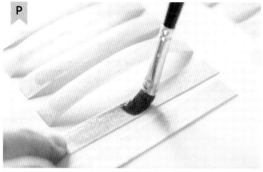

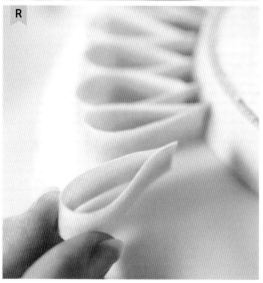

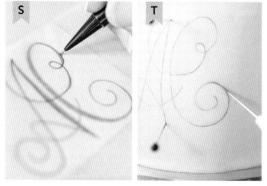

## THE PINK EDIBLE PAPER COLLAR

**1.** Dowel the base cake (see Dowelling Cakes) then attach the polystyrene separator using royal icing.

**2.** Take some pink edible wafer (rice) paper and, using a straight edge and a craft knife, cut around forty 1.5 x 8cm (⅝ x 3¼in) rectangles.

**3.** Arrange the rectangles, smooth side up, on clean white paper. Then use a paintbrush and piping gel to paint over each strip **(P)**. You will find that the added moisture makes the strips pop up away from the paper – this is perfectly normal! Leave the strips to dry for a few minutes.

**4.** Individually pick up the strips and bend them over to form loops, securing the ends with piping gel **(Q)**. Set aside to dry.

**5.** Once the loops have set, arrange them around the separator on the cake **(R)**, using piping gel to secure them in place.

## THE TOP TIER MONOGRAM

**1.** First, you will need to create your monogram, which is fairly straightforward using your computer. If you would like something a little more special than the fonts your computer has to offer, you can pay someone design a monogram for you. There are various websites that offer this service.

**2.** Resize your monogram to fit the top tier. Mine is approximately 6.5cm x 4.5cm (2½ x 1¾in).

**3.** Cut a 7.5cm (3in) wide strip of greaseproof (wax) paper to fit around your top tier. Position the monogram under the paper so the top is near the top of the strip, then trace over the design with a pencil **(S)**.

**4.** Secure the traced monogram to the front of the top tier with dressmakers' pins. Use a scriber to score the outline of the monogram onto the cake to aid placement **(T)**.

**5.** To soften the black modelling paste, knead it with some white vegetable fat (shortening), then dunk the paste into cooled boiled water and re-knead it. Repeat until the paste feels really soft and stretchy.

**6.** Place the softened black modelling paste together with the no. 1.5 piping tube into the sugar shaper and squeeze out lengths of paste onto your work surface. Leave the lengths to firm up so they can be handled easily, without breaking.

**7.** Paint sugar glue over the scored outline of the monogram. Take one of the lengths of paste and position it to follow the outline of one of the scored lines of the monogram **(U)**. Repeat for the remaining lines. Where the lines cross one another, decide which line you would like to be uppermost, then cut the paste at either side **(V)** and remove the segment not required.

**8.** Select areas of your monogram that you would like to enhance, then use your fluid writer and black liquid food colour to add colour to these additional areas **(W)**. Where you position these areas will depend upon the design of your monogram.

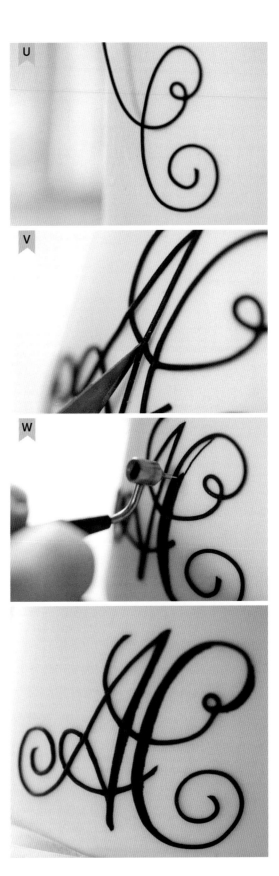

## PERFECT PLACEMENT

You may wish to experiment with the exact placement of the middle tier before securing it with royal icing.

## THE EDIBLE PAPER BOW

**1.** Use a ruler and craft knife to cut two 1.5cm (⅝in) wide strips from pink edible wafer (rice) paper. Place the strips onto clean white paper with their textured side uppermost.

**2.** Paint over the textured side of the strips with piping gel. Position one of the strips around the base of the top cake; the gelled side will need to face the cake, as the piping gel acts as a glue. Press on the strip to make sure it is well secured, adding more piping gel to the ends if necessary. The paper will initially have a tendency to curl away from the cake, but don't panic, as it can easily be encouraged to stay in place. Position the next strip, abutting one end against the first strip and cut to size with scissors.

**3.** Cut two more 1.5cm (⅝in) strips from pink edible paper, cutting one to a length of 16cm (6¼in). Mark the centre of this strip; this will create the loops of the bow. Place the strips onto clean white paper with their smooth side uppermost.

**4.** Paint over the top surface of the strips with piping gel. Pick up the strip with the marked centre and fold the ends into the mark **(X)** to create two evenly sized loops.

**5.** To make the bow centre, wrap the last strip around the centre of the bow **(Y)**, cutting off the excess at the back. Use piping gel to attach the bow centrally under the monogram, as shown.

## Assembling the cake

**1.** Dowel the middle tier (see Dowelling Cakes). If your cake is exceptionally heavy, you will also need to dowel the polystyrene spacer.

**2.** Using royal icing, attach the top tier to the middle tier. Use a set square to align the monogram and bow with the centre of the doodled design **(Z)**.

**3.** Attach the base tier to the covered board and the middle tier to the separator. Use the non-toxic glue stick to secure the ribbon to the edge of the cake board. Finally, add the prepared pink hybrid musk rose (see Edible Paper Flowers) to the top of your cake using a dot of royal icing or a posy pick.

# Two-tiered Doodle Design

If you are making this cake for a smaller number of guests, this scaled-back design is ideal. Use the same techniques as for the main cake to create the doodled flowers and monogram design, then simply finish with an elegant edible paper bow.

# Doodle and Bow Cookies

With Lindy's present cookie cutter (LC), bake and decorate the cookies using the techniques and equipment from the main cake. Create the bow from pink modelling paste using the patchwork cutter bow set, following the manufacturer's instructions. They make a sweet little gift to delight your wedding guests.

# FABULOUS FRINGES

## SERVES 102

*This* pretty, textured wedding cake was initially inspired by a fiery red and black Latino dance costume, bursting with movement and flamboyant fringes. Fringes are no longer confined to the edges of vintage lampshades; they can be found popping up everywhere, and the wedding scene is no exception. From long, single-layered fringes that sweep the floor to short multi-layered details on skirts, sleeves and bodices, fringes are a popular adornment on contemporary bridal gowns. With sugar fringing topped with a delicate floral band, bright aqua-textured ribbon details, a touch of lace and a striking edible flower topper, this tiered cake combines elegant modern style with a retro vintage influence.

For each tier, I wanted to achieve a unique layered effect using a number of techniques. A sugar shaper was used to create the fringing around the base, which I finished with an intricate floral band, made using a variety of cutters and stamps. By cutting and carefully folding strips of modelling paste, I created a textured ribbon effect on the second tier, and the third tier was embellished with gorgeous lace detail – surprisingly simple to make using an edible lace mix and mat. Finally, I topped the cake with a coordinating edible paper flower for a beautiful finishing touch. Why not experiment by mixing and matching the tiers?

# You will need

## CAKES

Bake, layer and stack your choice of cakes to create the following tier sizes:

- **base tier:** 25cm (10in) round, 9cm (3½in) deep

- **second tier:** 20cm (8in) round, 5.5cm (2¼in) deep

- **third tier:** 15cm (6in) round, 14.5cm (5¾in) deep

- **top tier:** 10cm (4in) round, 9cm (3½in) deep

## MATERIALS

- **sugarpaste (rolled fondant):** 500g (1lb 2oz) pale aqua; 1.5kg (3lb 5oz) aqua; 550g (1lb 4oz) brilliant white; 800g (1lb 12oz) pale green

- gum tragacanth or CMC (Tylose)

- 120g (4½oz) bright aqua modelling paste

- royal icing

- white vegetable fat (shortening)

- sugar glue

- white hundreds and thousands (nonpareils)

- edible lace mix

- basic punched flower (see Edible Paper Flowers)

- piping gel

## EQUIPMENT

- **round hardboard cake boards:** 15cm (6in); plus one the same size as each cake

- **polystyrene cake spacers:** 15cm (6in) round, 4cm (1½in) deep; or three 15cm (6in) round, 12mm (½in) deep cake drums

- scriber

- sugar shaper

- no. 2 piping tube (tip) (PME)

- Dresden tool

- card

- set square

- palette knife

- 1mm (¹⁄₃₂in) spacers

- **cutters:** Lindy's eight petal micro flower (LC); blossom plunger cutters – set of four (PME); Lindy's small Moroccan tile cutter (LC)

- foam pad

- ball tool

- paintbrush

- 1.4cm (⅝in) daisy centre stamp (JEM)

- craft knife

- **lace mats:** dentelle; leaf (SM)

- side scraper

- kitchen paper (paper towel)

- pearl-headed dressmakers' pin

- **dowels:** at least 15cm (6in) in length

- white edible wafer (rice) paper

## COLOURS

All the colours used on the cake have been created using Vine and Hydrangea (SK) paste colours.

### GET BAKING!

Find delicious cake recipes, suitable for decorating, in many of my previous books and on my blog.

### FREE THE FRINGE

The polystyrene cake separator is important in this design, as it allows space for the fringing to hang freely below the base of the cake.

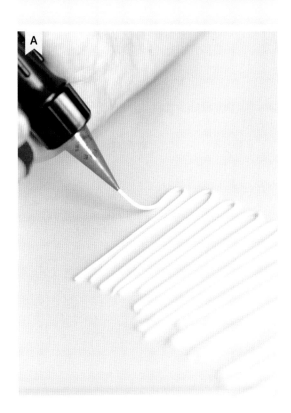

## Covering the cakes and spacer

Cover each of the cakes in turn (see Covering Cakes and Boards). Use Method 3 to cover the base tier with aqua sugarpaste and the second tier with brilliant white sugarpaste, covering the sides first and then the top. Cover the sides of the polystyrene spacer with aqua sugarpaste, again using Method 3. Cover the third tier with pale green sugarpaste using Method 4. Finally, cover the top tier with pale aqua sugarpaste using Method 1.

### MAKING THE MODELLING PASTE

Use the sugarpaste trimmings to make 300g (10½oz) aqua, 15g (½oz) pale aqua, 30g (1oz) pale green and 15g (½oz) brilliant white modelling paste by kneading in 1 tsp of gum tragacanth or CMC to every 225g (8oz) of sugarpaste.

## Decorating the cakes

### BASE TIER

THE FRINGING

**1.** Use a scriber to mark placement lines around the cake at 4cm (1½in) and 7.5cm (3in) heights.

**2.** Use royal icing to attach the covered polystyrene cake separator centrally to the underside of the base tier.

**3.** To make the loops for the fringe you will first need to soften some aqua modelling paste. Add a little white vegetable fat (shortening) to the paste to prevent it from getting too sticky, then dunk the paste into a container of cooled boiled water and knead to incorporate. Repeat until the modelling paste feels soft and stretchy.

**4.** Insert the softened paste into the barrel of the sugar shaper and add the piping tube (tip). Push the plunger down to remove any air and then pump the handle to squeeze out 8cm (3¼in) loops of soft paste onto your work surface **(A)**. Continue until the barrel is empty.

**5.** To make the loops more uniformly shaped, pinch the open ends together with your fingers, while using a Dresden tool to gently pull the looped ends away **(B)**.

**6.** Create a placement guide by folding a piece of card to 2cm (¾in) in height and placing it beneath the base of the cake. This will help to ensure that all loops hang at roughly the same height. Paint sugar glue 1cm (⅜in) above and below the lower marked line on the cake and start attaching the loops as shown **(C)**. Use a set square to gently push the loops closer together and to check they are hanging vertically **(D)**.

**7.** Once you have attached the first batch of loops, use a palette knife to cut away the ends at an angle above the lower marked line **(E)**. Repeat until the first row of loops is complete.

**8.** To make the second row of overlapping loops, make a 6cm (2⅜in) placement guide and repeat Steps 3–7, this time using the upper marked line **(F)**.

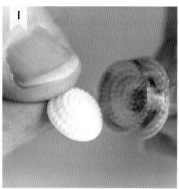

## CLEAR CUT

If any modelling paste remains in your cutter when it is lifted, wipe over the cutting edge with a finger, then push out the paste shape with a paintbrush.

## STAMP IT OUT

When using the stamp, add just enough paste to fill the mould, without the paste spilling out over the edges.

THE FLORAL BAND

**1.** To create the small eight-petal flowers, roll out some aqua modelling paste between 1mm (1/32in) spacers. Press the eight-petal micro flower cutter into the paste and give it a little wiggle before removing the cutter and excess paste **(G)**. Repeat to make about 30 flowers.

**2.** Place the cut-out flowers on a foam pad by gently stroking each petal with a ball tool to curve **(H)**. Place one cupped flower inside another, add a small white or aqua paste ball into the centre of each flower.

**3.** Use a large blossom plunger cutter to cut out five petal blossoms from thinly rolled-out aqua modelling paste – you will need about 20. Roll a ball of white modelling paste and press it firmly into the daisy centre stamp. By pressing your finger against the mould the paste should come away cleanly **(I)**. Repeat with the white and pale green modelling paste to make a centre for each flower and attach them in place using sugar glue.

**4.** Use the smallest blossom cutter to cut out a selection of brilliant white and bright aqua blossoms, then cup each one using a ball tool. Use the remaining cutters to create a selection of slightly larger blossoms, as shown in **(J)**.

**5.** Using sugar glue and a paintbrush, attach the flowers to the top edge of the cake, as desired, to create an attractive floral band **(K)**. To finish, add white hundreds and thousands (nonpareils) with a little sugar glue **(L)**.

## SECOND TIER

### RIBBONS

**1.** Thinly roll out some bright aqua modelling paste between 1mm (¹⁄₃₂in) spacers. Using a straight edge and a craft knife, cut strips measuring approximately 8mm (⁵⁄₁₆in) wide **(M)**.

**2.** Gently fold a strip of paste in half lengthways **(N)** and repeat for the remaining strips.

**3.** Paint sugar glue around the lower quarter of the covered cake. Starting at the base, secure the folded sugar ribbons in lines around the cake **(O)**. Use a Dresden tool to aid placement of the ribbons and encourage movement in the paste.

**4.** Continue cutting, folding and attaching the sugar ribbons, working up the cake until it is completely covered. Use a finger and a Dresden tool to make any necessary final adjustments to the pattern **(P)**.

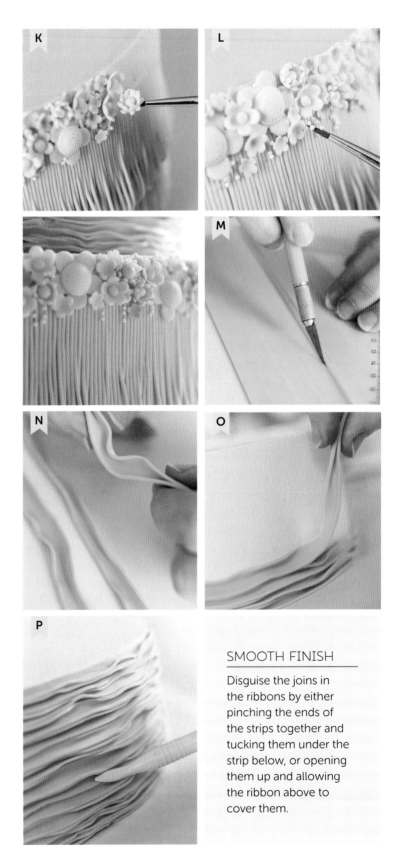

### SMOOTH FINISH

Disguise the joins in the ribbons by either pinching the ends of the strips together and tucking them under the strip below, or opening them up and allowing the ribbon above to cover them.

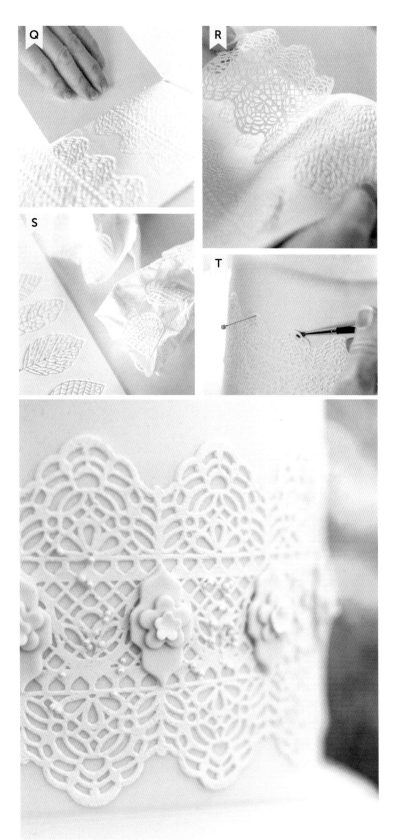

## THIRD TIER

### THE LACE

**1.** Mix up approximately 35g (1¼oz) of the edible lace mix, following the manufacturer's instructions. Use a side scraper to carefully spread the mixture over the dentelle and leaf lace mats **(Q)**. Dry in a cool oven or leave to air dry in a warm place.

**2.** Once the lace has dried sufficiently, carefully peel it away from the two lace mats **(R)**. Arrange the lace leaves in natural curved shapes on some scrunched-up kitchen paper and leave to dry further **(S)**.

**3.** Turn one section of the dried dentelle lace over and slightly dampen the underside of the lace. Using a dressmakers' pin to help hold the lace in place, wrap the lace centrally around the middle of the cake. Cut to fit with scissors and then secure the edges of the lace using a damp paintbrush **(T)** and applying a little pressure.

**4.** Use the small Moroccan tile cutter to cut tiles from thinly rolled-out green modelling paste and attach at regular intervals to the central lace band, as shown. Add aqua and white flowers to the centre of each tile in the same way as before (see The Floral Band). To finish, use sugar glue to randomly add a scattering of white hundreds and thousands (nonpareils) between the tiles.

## Assembling the cake

### TOP TIER

**1.** Dowel all the cakes, except the top tier (see Dowelling Cakes).

**2.** Stack the cakes (see Stacking Cakes), using royal icing to secure the tiers and referring to the finished cake for reference. Check the alignment and levels as you work.

**3.** Cut twelve 3mm (⅛in) wide ribbon strips from white edible paper (rice) sheets. Make the paper ribbons longer by joining two strips together with a little water. With the smooth, shiny side uppermost, wrap a paper ribbon around the base of the third tier (the lace tier), secure with piping gel and cut to size with a craft knife. Wrap another paper ribbon around the base of the top tier, then add a further four above. For these ribbons, start at the join and wrap the paper ribbons at increasing angles to the horizontal, leaving a small gap between each one to create the pattern shown on the finished cake.

### THE EDIBLE PAPER FLOWER

**1.** Following the instructions given, make the basic punched flower (see Edible Paper Flowers).

**2.** Roll a ball of white sugarpaste, attach it to the back of the edible paper flower and secure the flower onto the cake at the point where the paper ribbons meet.

**3.** Insert a few lace leaves into the ball of sugarpaste to help frame the flower.

# Floral Lace Mini Cakes

Embellish these 5cm (2in) mini cakes with delicate lace borders, made using the dentelle leaf mat and edible lace mix (see The Lace, Steps 1–3) and trimmed to size. Create a variety of floral elements using the same cutters and stamps as the main cake (see The Floral Band) to adorn part of the top section for a delicate finishing touch.

# BRIDAL VOGUE

## SERVES 50

*Inspired* by the latest in haute couture, fresh from the catwalk, this four-tiered design takes its inspiration from a number of fabulously innovative outfits and turns them into a head-turning, high-fashion wedding cake. The bold purple tier is scattered with striking flowers in different colours and styles, which are fun and easy to make using moulds. The repeating pattern on the bottom tier is created using a stencil and can easily be substituted with any design of your choice. With colour, texture and bags of style, this is the perfect cake for the bridal couple that definitely want to make a statement!

*I* love the mix of textures on this cake, from the ruched fabric effect on the white tier to the simple moulded flowers and embossed, delicate daisy leaves on the purple tier. The striking geometric pattern on the base gives the design a contemporary feel and is created using dust food colours, a retro circle stencil and a square cutter. The squares are carefully positioned with the help of a placement template and then framed by piping small dots of purple royal icing.

## You will need

### CAKES

Bake, layer and stack your choice of cakes to create the following tier sizes:

★ **base tier:** 20cm (8in) round, 7.5cm (3in) deep

★ **second tier:** 17cm (6¾in) round, 2cm (¾in) deep

★ **third tier:** 12cm (4¾in) round, 15cm (6in) deep

★ **top tier:** 7.5cm (3in) round, 5cm (2in) deep

### MATERIALS

★ **sugarpaste (rolled fondant):** 1kg (2lb 4oz) pale orange (SK Berberis); 800g (1lb 12oz) purple (MT Perfect Purple); 350g (12oz) white with a tint of pink

★ **modelling paste:** 50g (1¾oz) pale orange; 25g (1oz) purple; 25g (1oz) lilac; 25g (1oz) light lilac; 25g (1oz) white with a tint of pink; 50g (1¾oz) dark rusty orange; 50g (1¾oz) deep red-pink; 25g (1oz) dark green; 25g (1oz) light green, 25g (1oz) white

★ edible food dusts: purple (SK Violet); pink (SK Fuchsia)

★ sugar glue

★ royal icing

### EQUIPMENT

★ **cake boards:** 25cm (10in) round cake drum; round hardboards the same size as each cake

★ 1mm (¹⁄₃₂in) spacers

★ **flower moulds:** daisy mould set (FI – FL288); mini misc flower mould (FI – FL107)

★ ball tool

★ palette knife

★ Dresden tool

★ **cutters:** 4cm (1½in) square (FMM geometric set); daisy chain and leaf from large daisy (both PC)

★ craft knife

★ greaseproof (wax) paper

★ removable tape

★ paintbrush

★ set square

★ scriber

★ smoother

★ retro circle stencil (DS – C831)

★ reusable piping bag and coupler

★ **piping tubes (tips):** nos. 1, 2 (PME)

★ 80cm (31½in) length of 1.5cm (⅝in) wide bronze ribbon

★ non-toxic glue stick

★ **dowels:** at least 18cm (7in) in length

### COLOURS

### HARDBOARD HINT

Remember to place a hardboard cake board beneath each tier before covering.

### NOT TOO MUCH!

The white modelling paste should just line the centre section of the mould so it doesn't spread into the surrounding area when the purple modelling paste is added.

# Covering the cakes and board

**1.** Cover each of the cakes in turn as follows (see Covering Cakes with Sugarpaste). Cover the base and top tiers with pale orange sugarpaste using Method 1. Use Method 4 to cover the third tier with purple sugarpaste.

**2.** Cover the second tier with the tinted white sugarpaste using Method 1, making sure the finish around the bottom edge is neat. Take a straight edge – a 1mm (¹⁄₃₂in) spacer is ideal – and repeatedly indent close vertical and slightly off-vertical lines around the sides of the cake for a ruched fabric effect **(A)**.

**3.** Texture the top surface of the cake in a radial pattern from the centre **(B)**. Finally, join the two textured surfaces together by repeatedly rocking the straight edge over the top edge of the cake **(C)**. Set aside to dry.

# Decorating the cakes

### THE THIRD TIER

MAKING THE FLOWERS

**1.** To make the purple daisies – you can make three at a time with the suggested daisy mould – knead a small amount of white modelling paste to warm it. Roll three balls of paste, smaller than the centres of the largest daisies, and press the balls into the centre of each mould using a ball tool **(D)**.

**2.** Roll a ball of purple modelling paste, slightly larger than the daisy mould cavity. Push the ball of paste firmly into the mould, ensuring that the surface facing the mould is perfectly smooth.

**3.** Remove any excess paste with a palette knife so the back of the mould is just slightly domed. Using a Dresden tool, draw the excess paste between the petals into the centre, to ensure that the edge of each petal is properly defined **(E)**. Repeat for all three daisies.

**4.** Carefully flex the mould to release the moulded daisies **(F)**. If the white centres have spread to the surrounding petals, you will need to add less paste into the centre next time.

**5.** To create the large pale orange daisies, start by adding a small ball of purple modelling paste to the centre of the daisy mould. Use a ball tool to spread the paste to just line the centre of the mould **(G)**. Place a small ball of white modelling paste over the purple centre and use the pointed end of a Dresden tool to spread the white paste very thinly around the base of the petals **(H)**.

**6.** Next add the pale orange modelling paste to completely fill the mould, removing any excess paste with a palette knife **(I)**. Press the mould firmly to ensure each petal is filled. Carefully flex the mould to release the flower.

## DAISY DETAIL

If you are not getting enough detail on your daisies, check that you are pressing firmly enough and that your modelling paste is not too stiff.

**7.** To finish the flower, take the pointed end of the Dresden tool and carefully scrape the white modelling paste back towards the centre, to remove any hard lines and give a feathery appearance **(J)**.

**8.** Using the same techniques with the suggested moulds and various colours of modelling paste, create a selection of different flowers as shown **(K)**.

MAKING THE LEAVES

**1.** Knead the dark green modelling paste until it is warm and pliable. Thinly roll it out onto your work surface and leave it for a few moments. Press the daisy leaf cutter firmly into the paste and give it a little 'wiggle'. Remove the cutter and repeat **(L)**. Make the smaller leaves using the daisy chain cutter. Remove the excess paste and allow the leaves to firm up for a minute or two.

**2.** Using sugar glue, attach the moulded flowers and cut-out leaves to the cake, referring to the finished cake for guidance on placement. The vertical join in the sugarpaste can easily be disguised with strategically placed flowers and leaves.

LOVELY LEAVES

The cutter should cut out the leaves and emboss the veins; if it does not, try rolling the modelling paste a little thinner.

## THE BASE TIER

### CREATING THE SQUARE PATTERN

**1.** Make a placement guide to position the squares evenly around your cake. Do this by accurately measuring the diameter of your covered base cake. Using a craft knife and straight edge, cut a strip of greaseproof (wax) paper 1cm (⅜in) wide x your cake diameter measurement, plus a little extra. Divide the diameter of your cake by ten and mark this measurement ten times onto the strip.

**2.** Place the paper strip around the cake and use removable tape to temporarily secure it. Take a set square and a scriber and make two marks: one just above the paper and the other vertically above this at a height of 6.5cm (2½in) **(M)**. Leave the paper in place for the time being.

**3.** Roll out some of the pale orange modelling paste using 1mm (⅟₃₂in) spacers. Place the retro circle stencil on top and press down firmly with a smoother to prevent the stencil from moving.

**4.** Next mix the pink and purple dust food colours to create a warm purple shade. Dip a paintbrush into the dust food colour, knock off any excess, then carefully dust over the stencil **(N)**, varying the intensity of colour slightly by adding more or less dust to various sections of the pattern.

**5.** Use a dry paintbrush to remove any excess dust from the stencil: this will ensure that no stray dust falls from the stencil as you lift it, spoiling the pattern beneath. Carefully lift the stencil away from the paste to reveal the pattern **(O)**. Pick up the stencilled paste and place it on a clean section of your work surface to prevent the paste from sticking to your work board.

## DESIGN ALTERNATIVES

Try experimenting with other food grade stencils to see if you prefer an alternative design.

**6.** Take the square cutter and carefully position it centrally over the pattern. Once you are happy with the placement, press down on the cutter and remove it, together with any excess paste **(P)**. Repeat to make nine more squares.

**7.** Making sure your hands are spotlessly clean, turn a square over and dampen the back with water or sugar glue. Attach to the cake, using the marked dots and the placement guide to help you. Repeat for the remaining nine squares, removing the paper placement guide once you have finished.

**8.** Colour some royal icing a deep purple and adjust the consistency of the icing: you want to be piping dots, not pointed cones. Fit a no. 2 piping tube (tip) into a small reusable piping (pastry) bag fitted with a coupler and half fill with freshly paddled, smooth royal icing. Supporting your hand, either on your work surface or turntable, hold the tip fractionally above the cake surface on one of the points of a square. Squeeze the bag until the icing dot is the required size, release the pressure and only then remove the tip: this helps to avoid any unwanted peaks. Remember: squeeze, release and then lift. Repeat to pipe a dot at each corner of every square **(Q)**.

**9.** Replace the piping tube with a no. 1 tube and pipe evenly spaced dots along the sides of each square **(R)**. Allow to dry.

## Assembling the cake

**1.** Using royal icing, attach the base tier to the centre of the cake board.

**2.** Roll out a 3–4cm (1¼–1½in) wide strip of pale orange sugarpaste and cut one edge straight. Dampen the top surface of the board with water then, starting at the back, carefully position the cut edge of the strip around the cake **(S)**, cutting the length to fit. Trim any excess from the edge of the board, using a palette knife to get a clean, vertical cut **(T)**.

**3.** Dowel all except the top tier (see Dowelling Cakes), then stack the cakes (see Stacking Cakes), using royal icing to secure. Check alignment and levels as you go and refer to the finished cake for guidance. Attach the ribbon to the edge of the cake board using a non-toxic glue stick.

# Floral Fashion Cupcakes

Beautiful tiered swirls of fluffy buttercream and a moulded flower top these stylish cupcakes, baked in rich purple cases (liners). Colour the buttercream to match the cake colours, ensuring it is the correct consistency and temperature: too stiff and cold and it will be hard to pipe; too soft and warm and it won't retain its shape.

Place peach-coloured buttercream and a Wilton 1M or similar piping tube (tip) into a large piping (pastry) bag. Holding the piping bag vertically and starting at the centre, apply pressure to the bag then move the tube to the edge of the cupcake and move around the centre in an anticlockwise direction, holding the tube above the cake surface so the icing falls in place. Once you have completed one full circle, release the pressure and remove the piping bag. Make the smaller white top tier in the same way, using a Wilton 6B or similar piping tube. Finally, top with a moulded flower, made in the same way as for the main cake.

# GLITZ AND GLAMOUR

## SERVES 62

**Extravagant** and sensational, this wedding cake will add a fabulous touch of style to a very special occasion. Inspired by feathery wedding dress details, sumptuous lace and colourful statement embroidery, the chic design is a wonderful mixture of old and new. Floating on the frivolous feathery white cloud of the base tier, the pink central tier makes a wonderfully bold statement, drawing the eye towards the piped and painted detail. The topper, with its ordered yet chaotic loops, tops the cake beautifully and creates balance and harmony between the tiers.

This striking abstract flower is embossed onto the middle tier as soon as it is covered with sugarpaste. The outlines are piped with royal icing, which is brushed immediately with a damp paintbrush, spreading the icing in long strokes that lightly fill each petal. Colour is then added and random dots are piped to finish the look. I used steam to give the layered edible paper strips on the base tier movement for a three-dimensional feathered effect. The delicate lace is simple to make by spreading a lace mix over a baroque lace mat and the twisted edible paper strips create a fun and frivolous topper.

## You will need

### CAKES

Bake, layer and stack your choice of cakes to create the following tier sizes:

★ **base tier:** 20cm (8in) round, 8.5cm (3⅜in) deep

★ **second tier:** 15cm (6in) round, 15cm (6in) deep

★ **top tier:** 10cm (4in) round, 6cm (2⅜in) deep

### MATERIALS

★ **sugarpaste (rolled fondant):** 1.1kg white (2lb 7oz); 800g (1lb 12oz) pink

★ royal icing

★ edible white wafer (rice) paper

★ edible lace mix

★ **liquid food colours:** peach (SK Nasturtium); purple (SK Violet)

★ piping gel

### EQUIPMENT

★ **cake boards:** 28cm (11in) round cake drum; round hardboards the same size as each cake

★ Lindy's designer petal cutter set (LC)

★ palette knife

★ **piping tubes (tips):** nos. 1.5, 2 (PME)

★ small reusable piping (pastry) bag and coupler

★ craft knife

★ small scissors

★ no. 4 paintbrush

★ baroque lace mat (SM)

★ side scraper

★ pearl-headed dressmakers' pins

★ tilting turntable (optional)

★ white paper

★ **dowels:** at least 16cm (6¼in) in length

★ 90cm (35½in) length of 1.5cm (⅝in) wide white ribbon

★ non-toxic glue stick

### COLOURS

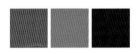

For the middle tier, Lindy used Pretty Pink sugarpaste (MT) and Ruby (SF) paste colours.

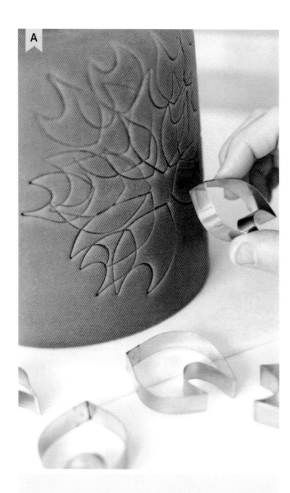

## Covering the cakes and board

**1.** Place the cakes onto their hardboards, then cover each in turn as follows (see Covering Cakes with Sugarpaste). Use white sugarpaste to cover the base cake using Method 2, the top tier using Method 1 and then cover the cake drum (see Covering Boards).

**2.** Cover the middle tier with pink sugarpaste using Method 4. Then immediately emboss the abstract flower pattern onto the front of the cake. Do this by taking the set of designer petal cutters and pressing the shapes firmly into the soft paste to create the petal outlines, using the finished cake as a placement guide **(A)**. Place to one side to dry.

## Decorating the cake

### THE BASE TIER

#### THE DOTTED BORDER

**1.** Centrally position the cake onto the covered cake board, using a little royal icing to secure it.

**2.** Paddle some soft-peak royal icing, using a palette knife to expel all the air bubbles. Then, if necessary, add a few drops of cooled boiled water to make a perfectly smooth icing. To pipe dots, place a no. 2 piping tube (tip) into a small piping (pastry) bag and half fill with the smooth royal icing. Supporting your hand on your work surface, hold the tube fractionally above the join between the cake and the board. Squeeze the bag until the dot is of a suitable size, release the pressure and only then remove the tube; this will help to avoid any unwanted peaks. Leave a small gap and repeat until you have small dots of an even size going all the way around the base of your cake **(B)**. Remember: squeeze, release and then lift.

## PRACTICE FIRST

Practise embossing your pattern onto some spare paste before you start to work on the cake.

## THE FEATHERING

**1.** Stack four sheets of white edible (rice) paper on top of each other on a suitable cutting surface. Using a ruler and craft knife, cut 3cm (1¼in) wide strips **(C)**. You will need between 15 and 20 strips, depending on how many layers you wish to add.

**2.** Pick up four strips of edible paper and use small sharp scissors to repeatedly cut into the strips along their long edges to create the feathering effect **(D)**. Repeat for the remaining strips.

**3.** To add movement to the feathering you will need a steady source of steam. I used a saucepan with its lid at a slight angle to direct the steam, brought to the boil on full power and then turned down by about a third. If you use too much steam, the edible paper just melts; too little and you will not add any movement. Pick up one of the edible paper feathered strips and, with the rough side uppermost, hold part of the strip over the steam **(E)**. You will notice that the feathering starts to move, curl and take on a life of its own. At this point remove the strip: once it is away from the steam, the paper becomes rigid again very quickly! Repeat until the whole strip has been steamed. If you are unhappy with the shape of any section, simply place it back under the steam and wait for it to reshape. Repeat for all remaining strips.

**4.** To attach the strips, first paint over the sides of the cake with cooled boiled water. Position a feathered strip on the side of the cake so the tips of the feathers rest on the covered cake board. To secure the strip, take a clean dry paintbrush and press where necessary onto the top part of the strips to ensure a good contact is made between the two surfaces.

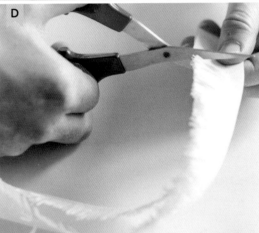

## SAFETY FIRST

Take care when using this technique: steam can burn!

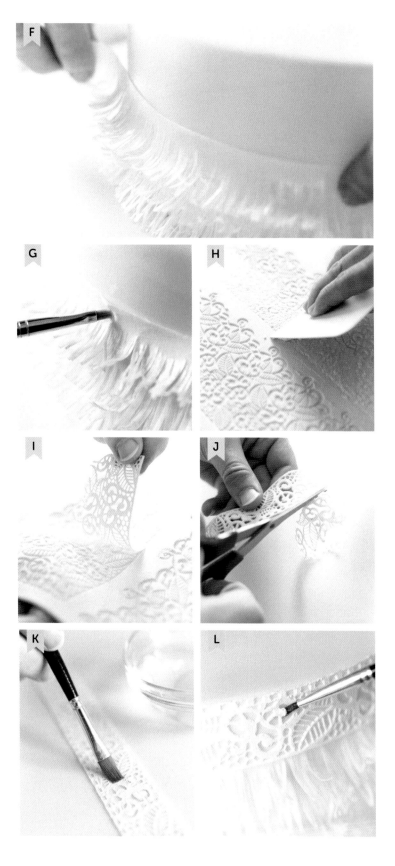

**5.** Continue adding feather strips around the cake **(F)**, securing each one with a clean dry paintbrush **(G)**, cutting the last one to size on each layer as required. I have created five layers of feathering, but you can easily add more or fewer, just remember to leave space for the lace!

THE LACE

**1.** Mix up approximately 35g (1¼oz) of the edible lace mix, following the manufacturer's instructions. Use a palette knife to spread the mixture over the lower half of the lace patterns on the lace mat, then take the side scraper and carefully remove the excess mix **(H)**. Dry in a cool oven at 70°C (158°F) or leave to air dry in a warm place.

**2.** Once the lace has dried sufficiently, carefully peel it away from the lace mat **(I)**. Next, take some scissors and cut all the way along the centre of the pattern to create two lace bands **(J)**.

**3.** Turn the lace over and slightly dampen the underside of each band using a paintbrush and water **(K)**. Using dressmakers' pins to help hold the lace in place, wrap the two pieces of lace end-to-end around the top edge of the cake. Cut to fit with scissors, then use a damp paintbrush to secure the edges and any protruding sections in the lace **(L)**, encouraging them to sit flush with the surface of the cake by using a little pressure. Remove all the pins.

## THE CENTRE TIER

**1.** Place the covered pink cake on a tilting turntable, or prop the cake up at an angle with the flower facing, but tilting away from you.

**2.** Place the no. 1.5 piping tube (tip) into your piping (pastry) bag and half fill with freshly prepared, smooth royal icing. You need to work from the background to the foreground, so choose one of the outer petals to begin with. Touch the cake surface at the top of a petal with the tip of the tube, and at the same time, lightly apply pressure to the bag. As the icing starts to flow, lift the tube away from the cake. When it is the length of the petal, release the pressure and position the icing along one embossed edge of a petal. Remember: touch, lift and then place.

**3.** Repeat for the other outer edge and curved top, then add a second layer to the curved top of the petal, as shown **(M)**.

**4.** Dampen a reasonably firm brush with cooled boiled water, blotting off any excess moisture with a paper towel. Place the brush on the wet icing and draw the icing from the top of the petal downwards using long strokes **(N)**. Once the top of the petal is complete, brush the icing on the sides and base of the petal in more or less the same direction as the top, as can be seen in the step photograph. When brushing through the icing, aim to keep the outer line unbroken; you can, however, add more icing if necessary.

**5.** Continue working around your embossed flower design, brushing each section as soon as you have piped it to prevent the icing drying out.

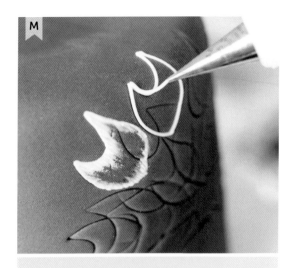

### EXTRA TIME

You may find that adding just a little piping gel to the royal icing will slow down the drying time, giving you more time to work on each petal.

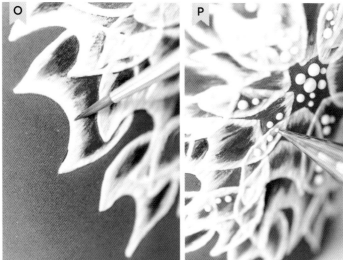

**6.** Once the royal icing has dried (this doesn't take long), take a fine-pointed paintbrush and dip it into the peach liquid food colour. Referring to the finished cake for guidance, use light feathered strokes in the direction of the brush embroidery to fill in sections of some of the petals **(O)**. Take a clean brush and paint other petal sections with the purple liquid food colour in the same way, then leave to dry.

**7.** Once the paint has dried, use your royal icing and piping tubes to pipe randomly spaced dots inside the flower design, as shown **(P)**.

## THE TOP TIER

**1.** Cut 5mm (¼in) wide strips from edible (rice) paper using a straight edge and craft knife. Place the strips onto clean white paper with their rough side uppermost. Paint each strip with piping gel to allow it to be twisted and shaped **(Q)**.

**2.** Pick up a strip and twist it, as shown **(R)**. Holding the twist, stick both ends to the top of the cake so that they are in the centre and the twist forms a rough figure of eight. Add the next strip in the same way, placing it at an angle to the first, as shown **(S)**.

**3.** Continue adding twisted strips **(T)** until you are happy with the effect.

## Assembling the cake

**1.** Dowel the base and middle tiers (see Dowelling Cakes). Using royal icing, attach the pink tier centrally to the base tier, checking the alignment and levels. Finally, add the top tier.

**2.** Attach a length of edible lace around the top tier, prepared and attached as for the base tier (see The Lace).

**3.** Secure the white ribbon to the edge of the cake board (see Covering Boards), using the non-toxic glue stick.

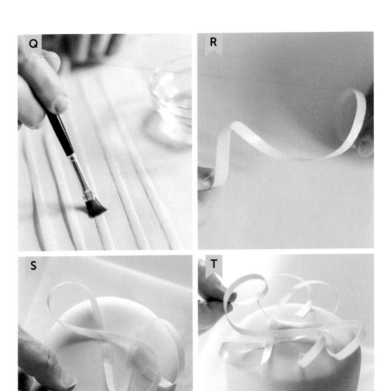

# Dress to Impress Cookies

These glamorous cookies are baked using Lindy's fitted dress and top hat cookie cutters (LC). Cover the party dresses with half pink and half white sugarpaste, then decorate using the same feathering, lace and embossing techniques used for the main cake.

To decorate the top hat cookie, separately roll out some grey sugarpaste to 5mm (¼in) and 3mm (⅛in) thicknesses. Use the cutter to cut out a top hat from each paste. Cut away the crown of the hat from its brim on each shape with a craft knife. Using piping gel, attach the 5mm (¼in) thick crown to the cookie, then smooth the crown sides with your fingers to give a rounded appearance. Emboss the top of the crown using a large circle cutter, then cut a 7mm (⁵⁄₁₆in) wide strip from black modelling paste and attach it in place, as shown. Next attach the 3mm (⅛in) thick brim, carefully placing it around the base of the crown. Finally, roll a tapered sausage to fit around the outer edge of the brim and attach in place.

# RADIANT RIBBONS

## SERVES 85

*Forget* traditional white and opt for this bright and colourful two-tired cake to give your wedding a truly modern feel. The flamboyant design, with its orange highlights, was originally inspired by a visit to the ultra-modern and distinctive Liverpool Metropolitan Cathedral. It combines elements of a large tapestry hanging high up above a side altar and the brightly coloured stained glass panels standing proudly outside the cathedral's entrance. If you dream of a colourful cake with bags of style and personality, this could be the perfect design for you!

This is one of my favourite designs and it is surprisingly simple to create. I have used a cutting wheel to emboss the flowing ribbon pattern over the base tier, which is quite straightforward, provided you have a turntable on which to place the cake. The colour is painted on by hand using a mixture of food paints, liquid colours and a paste colour. Darker paint colours predominate on the lower half of the tier with lighter, more pastel shades on the upper sections. The top tier is finished beautifully with a cream modelling paste ribbon and pretty punched flower.

# You will need

## CAKES

Bake, layer and stack your choice of cakes to create the following tier sizes:

★ **base tier:** 20cm (8in) round, 20cm (8in) deep

★ **second tier:** 15cm (6in) round, 9.5cm (3¾in) deep

## MATERIALS

★ **sugarpaste (rolled fondant):** 2kg (4lb 8oz) white; 150g (5½oz) dark blue

★ **modelling paste:** 100g (3½oz) cream; 150g (5½oz) white

★ **food paint:** Rainbow Dust: Paint It! – sky blue, spring green, turquoise

★ **liquid food colours:** dark peach (SK Berberis); peach (SK Nasturtium); tangerine (SK Marigold); yellow (SK Sunflower); dark blue (SK Hyacinth); green (SK Mint)

★ brown paste food colour (SK Terracotta)

★ royal icing

★ basic punched flower (see Edible Paper Flowers)

★ green edible wafer (rice) paper

## EQUIPMENT

★ **cake boards:** 23cm (9in) round cake drum; round hardboards the same size as each cake

★ turntable

★ cutting wheel (PME)

★ bulbous cone tool (PME)

★ selection of paintbrushes

★ smoother

★ 73cm (28¾in) length of 1.5cm (⅝in) wide teal green ribbon

★ non-toxic glue stick

★ **dowels:** at least 21cm (8¼in) in length

★ **spacers:** 1mm (¹⁄₃₂in); 5mm (¼in)

★ palette knife

★ craft knife

★ multi-ribbon cutter (FMM)

★ die-cutting machine

★ leaf die set (Xcut)

## COLOURS

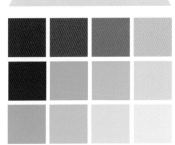

Hyacinth paste food colour (SK) was used for the dark blue sugarpaste on the cake board.

A

## HIDDEN JOIN

Don't worry too much about the join on the side of the cake; this can easily be disguised as part of the pattern.

## Covering the cakes

**1.** Place the hardboard beneath the top tier, then cover with white sugarpaste using Method 1 (see Covering Cakes with Sugarpaste) and set aside.

**2.** Place the hardboard beneath the bottom tier and cover using Method 5, covering the top first and then the sides. Once covered, place this cake onto a turntable.

## Embossing the pattern

**1.** Once you have covered the base tier, immediately – without allowing the sugarpaste to harden – add the embossed pattern. Use a cutting wheel and refer to the photographs of the completed cake for guidance – it's a lot simpler than you might think!

**2.** Start by drawing on the central 'S' shape that creates the 'stem' of the flower **(A)**. Then, starting at the top edge, add the shallow 'C' shapes at either side – these will be painted orange later. Add further 'S' and 'C' shapes, as desired, around the back and sides of the cake.

**3.** Next, add the diagonal sweeping strokes that run from top left to bottom right. Do this by placing your cutting wheel at the top of the cake at a 45° angle. Using your free hand, turn the turntable clockwise, whilst running your cutting wheel down the cake to the base in one long sweeping movement. Repeat at differing intervals until you have sweeping strokes circumventing the cake **(B)**.

**4.** Now add sweeping strokes running in the opposite direction by angling your cutting wheel from top right to bottom left and turning your turntable in an anticlockwise direction **(C)**.

**5.** Once you are happy that you have enough sweeping strokes, hold your cutting wheel in a vertical position and divide up the segments with vertical lines **(D)**. At this point, you can also clearly disguise the join in your sugarpaste by making vertical strokes over the join, so it becomes part of the pattern.

**6.** Finally, take a bulbous cone tool or similar and indent random dots into a few segments **(E)**. Once you are happy with your overall design, place the cake aside to allow the sugarpaste to crust over.

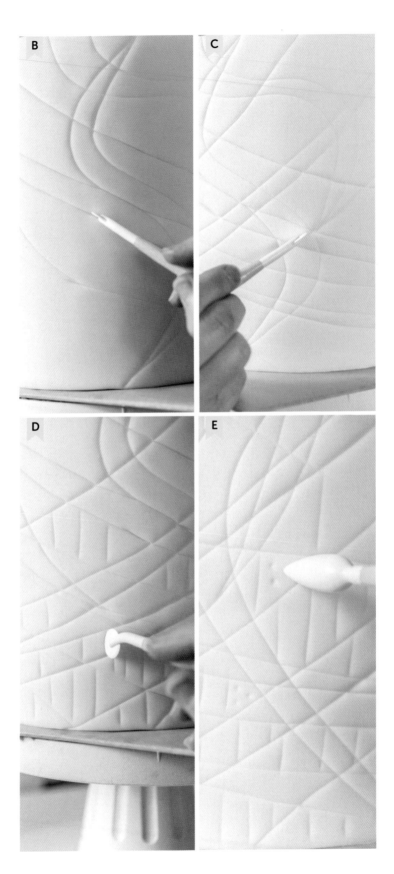

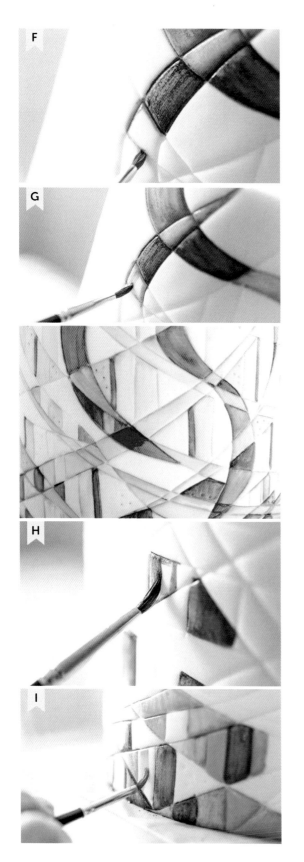

# Painting the cake

To paint the cake, I have used a mixture of food paint, liquid food colours and one paste food colour. Note: the food paints are the easiest to apply, so I would have opted just to use these if it was possible to mix them to the colours I wanted. However, liquid food colours are the next best thing. I used the paste food colour simply because I love using this particular colour straight out of the pot – it saves mixing time! To prevent your colours from becoming muddy, always use a clean brush when changing colours.

## ADDING THE ORANGE PAINT

**1.** First, you will need to decide on a segment to paint. I started with the central stem but you may prefer to practise on the back of the cake first! Load the brush with your choice of peach liquid food colouring and paint around the edges of your chosen segment, making sure the colour goes right into the bottom of the embossed line **(F)**.

**2.** Next fill in the segment using brush strokes that follow the line of the 'S' or 'C' shape **(G)**. If the painted segment looks a little dark, simply take a clean damp brush and remove some of the colour, again using strokes that follow the overall shape.

**3.** Continue changing the shade for each segment until all the 'S' and 'C' shapes have been painted.

## ADDING THE BLUE, GREEN AND BROWN PAINT

**1.** Starting at the base of the cake and referring to the photograph of the finished cake, use the dark blue (Hyacinth) liquid food colour to paint sections. Outline each shape, as before, then use vertical brushstrokes to fill them in **(H)**.

**2.** Next use the green (Mint) liquid food colour to paint segments around the dark blue sections on the lower third of the cake.

**3.** Now switch to the three food paints; painting with these is more like painting with poster paints, as they are much thicker. Use the paint neat or dilute it with a little water and fill in your selected segments as before **(I)**.

**4.** You will see from the completed cake that not all segments are painted and the colours become paler as they go up the cake. Create the pale segments by simply diluting both the liquid food colours and food paints with a little water and painting as before **(J)**.

**5.** Dilute the terracotta paste colour with water and add the final colour in two strengths: dilute for the larger segments and less dilute for the narrow vertical lines. Once you are happy with your painted cake, leave it to dry.

## Finishing the main tier

**1.** As the cake was covered in two sections, it is important to neaten the visible join at the top. You will probably find that the sugarpaste around the join is not completely flat, so to even this out, dilute it with some white sugarpaste. To do this, use a palette knife to mix cooled boiled water into the sugarpaste until it has a spreadable consistency, but is not sloppy. Using the palette knife, spread the icing over the join in the pastes, as shown **(K)**. Smooth the icing and place to one side.

**2.** Knead the white modelling paste to warm it and roll it out between 1mm (1/32in) spacers. Use a cake board or plate to cut out a circle, fractionally bigger than the top of the cake. Place the modelling paste circle on top of the cake and use a smoother in a circular action to level the top.

**3.** Next, take a craft knife and, holding it vertically, cut the circle to neatly fit the top of the cake. You will find that your circle isn't perfect, as your knife will follow the contours of the textured lines, but the overall appearance will be a neat edge.

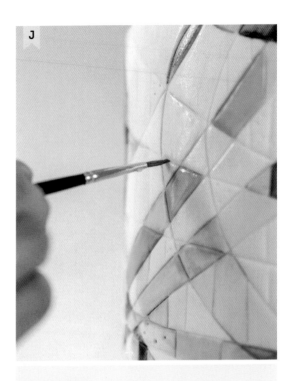

### DRYING HINT

Make sure you find a dry place to leave your cake; a moist atmosphere will prevent the paint from drying.

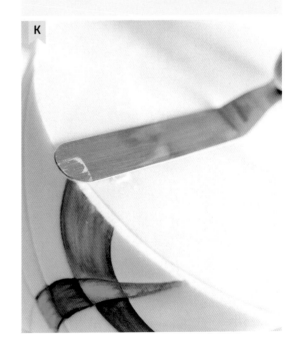

**4.** Place the cake centrally onto its cake board, using royal icing to secure.

**5.** Roll the dark blue sugarpaste into a long sausage between 5mm (¼in) spacers and cut it into a 72 × 1cm (28½ × ⅜in) strip. Wrap the paste around the cake; making sure the join is at the back. Smooth carefully with a smoother, then cut away any excess with a palette knife.

**6.** Finally, attach the ribbon around the edge of the cake board, using a non-toxic glue stick to secure.

## Decorating the top tier

### CREATING THE CREAM RIBBON

**1.** Dowel the base tier (see Dowelling Cakes) and securely place the top tier in position, checking that it is placed centrally and the cake is level.

**2.** Knead the cream modelling paste to warm it, then roll out into a long strip between 1mm (¹⁄₃₂in) spacers. Set the multi-ribbon cutter to a 3cm (1⅛in) width and use it to cut a 50cm (20in) length of ribbon from the cream modelling paste **(L)**. Allow the paste to firm up for a minute or two, so that it retains its shape.

**3.** Attach the cream paste ribbon around the base of the top tier so the join is at the front – at the top of the orange painted 'S' shape. Cut the paste to fit with a craft knife.

## ADDING THE FLOWER AND LEAVES

**1.** Roll a 2.5cm (1in) ball of white sugarpaste. Position it on top of the base tier at the point of the join in the ribbon on the top tier **(M)**.

**2.** Take the prepared petals and build the basic punched flower (see Edible Paper Flowers). Create the centre and secure it in place.

**3.** To make the leaves, cut two sheets of green edible (rice) paper to fit the plates of your die-cutting machine. Set up the die-cutter plates with the edible paper and leaf die, following the instructions for your machine. Place in your die cutter and turn the handle to cut out the leaves **(N)**. Release the leaves from the die **(O)**.

**4.** Attach the leaves in place on your cake using a little piping gel or water **(P)**.

## FREE THE LEAVES

If your leaves don't pop out easily, use the tip of a craft knife or scriber to help release them.

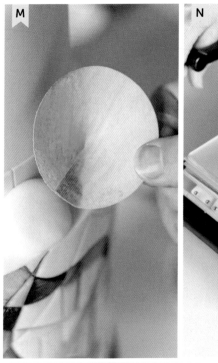

# Big Hat Cupcakes

These chic cupcakes are decorated using Lindy's fancy wedding hats stencils (LC). Bake a selection of cupcakes in blue and green paper cases (liners). Aim for a shallow dome – the sticky ginger recipe in the recipe section of my blog works well. Roll out white sugarpaste to a 5mm (¼in) thickness, ideally using spacers. Place a hat stencil on top of the sugarpaste and gently press down onto the stencil with a smoother to secure it in place.

Select and mix suitable dust food colours. Dip a soft brush into one of the dusts, knock off any excess, then carefully dust over small sections of the stencil, varying the intensity of colour by adding more or less dust. Take a clean brush, dip it into another colour and carefully dust over new sections of the hat. Repeat to add as many colours as you wish, then carefully lift the stencil away from the paste to reveal the completed hat. Using a circle cutter, the same size as the tops of your cupcakes, cut out the sugarpaste and position it on top.

# EDIBLE PAPER FLOWERS

*E*dible paper – also known as wafer paper, confectioner's paper or rice paper – is a highly versatile medium for decorating cakes. Although it has been available for decades, it is only recently that cake decorators have started using edible paper more creatively. I was introduced to the art of edible paper flower making by Stevi Auble, through her online Craftsy classes. I was intrigued, so started experimenting and soon found that the paper is easy to work with and I loved what I could create. For me, the beauty of using edible paper for flowers is that large impressive blooms can be made relatively quickly and they stand up really well in damp and humid conditions, which – for me, being in the UK – is important. I have also found edible paper flowers a lot less fragile than delicate sugar flowers; although if you live in a dry climate you might not agree!

# The paper

Sheets of edible paper, which are actually made from potato starch, have two distinctive sides: one smooth and one textured. At the time of writing, the paper is available in white and a small range of pastel colours. On the following pages I will show you how to colour the paper yourself, although you can also use an edible printer if you are lucky enough to have one.

## PAINTING ON EDIBLE PAPER

When painting edible paper, you will need to create an oil-based paint by mixing a little food colour dust with a small amount of vegetable oil. You will find that the paint is readily absorbed into the textured side of the edible paper, but not so easily applied into the smooth sides. You may also find that the distribution of colour can be uneven: don't worry, as this will change a little as the paint dries, and a slightly mottled appearance adds to the charm of the flowers.

## SHAPING THE PAPER

Straight from the packet, the paper is very brittle and can easily be snapped or torn. To make it more flexible and able to be shaped, I use a mixture of piping gel and steam, depending on the results I require. Please note that the art of creating edible paper flowers is very much in its infancy, so we are all experimenting. Some people simply use water to soften the paper but this didn't work well enough for me. My advice is to have fun experimenting yourself; try my techniques, try others and see which work best for you.

When using steam to shape petals, I have found it best to first paint the petals that you wish to shape with piping gel. Next, hold the gelled paper over your steam source. You will notice that the petals start to move and take on a life of their own – at this point remove them and manipulate your petals as desired. Once away from the steam, the petals become rigid again very quickly. However, if you are unhappy with the shape of any petal, simply place it back under the steam to reshape it.

### SUCCESS WITH STEAM

To help shape the paper and create some of the three-dimensional flowers, you will need a steady source of steam. The best method I found is to bring water to the boil on full power in a saucepan, then turn it down by about a third, keeping the lid at a slight angle to direct the steam. If you use too much steam, the edible paper just melts; too little, and it becomes impossible to manipulate the petals. Once you are familiar with the technique, a craft steamer might be a good investment. Remember, steam can burn, so take care.

# Basic punched flower

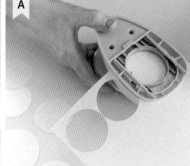

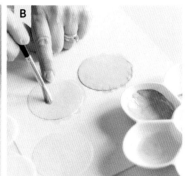

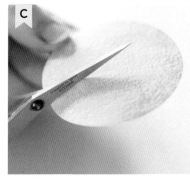

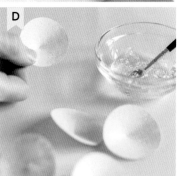

**W**hen simplicity and style are what you require, a punched flower is a fantastic, relatively quick way of making a large floral focal point.

## YOU WILL NEED

★ white edible wafer (rice) paper

★ circle punches: 6.5cm (2½in); 5cm (2in); 4cm (1¾in)

★ white paper

★ matt food colour dusts: blue (SK Hydrangea), lime green (SK Vine), white (SF Superwhite)

★ vegetable oil, e.g. sunflower

★ paintbrushes

★ scissors

★ piping gel

★ white sugarpaste (rolled fondant)

★ sugar glue (optional)

★ white hundreds and thousands (nonpareils)

## CREATING THE BASIC PUNCHED FLOWER

**1.** Using up to four sheets of edible paper at once, use the punches to punch out five circles of each size **(A)**. The number that you can cleanly cut at once will depend on the cutting edges of your punches.

**2.** Place the edible paper circles onto a clean sheet of white paper. Mix a small amount of the suggested food colour dusts with a little vegetable oil to create a selection of oil-based paint colours. For my aqua flower, I have used a mainly white base with a touch of blue and green to create three shades of one colour. Use the mixed oil-based paint to paint both sides of each circle **(B)** (see Painting on Edible Paper). With the textured side uppermost, add a slightly darker shade around the outer edges of the larger circle. Transfer the painted flowers with their textured side uppermost onto a fresh sheet of white paper and allow to dry.

**3.** Once the paint has dried, use scissors to cut into the centre of each circle **(C)**.

**4.** Pick up a large circle, overlap the cut edges to create a shallow cone and stick it in position using piping gel **(D)**. Repeat for each circle and leave to dry.

**5.** Once the petals have set in shape, roll a 2.5cm (1in) diameter ball of sugarpaste and place it either onto your work surface or directly onto the cake you are decorating. Using a

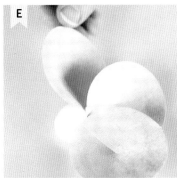

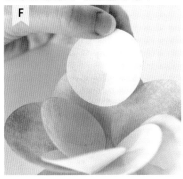

small amount of piping gel as a glue, attach the five large outer petals to the ball of paste **(E)**. Overlap the petals and tuck the last one under the first.

**6.** Repeat using the medium-sized petals **(F)** and finally the smallest petals. Adjust the positioning of the petals as necessary and once you are happy, allow them to set in place.

**7.** To create the centre, roll a small ball of white sugarpaste to your desired size and attach it to the centre of the dried flower. Cover the ball with sugar glue or piping gel, then carefully pour over some hundreds and thousands (nonpareils), tipping away the excess and adjusting their position as necessary. Allow to dry.

## MAKING AN ALTERNATIVE CENTRE

There are various methods of adding a centre to this basic flower and another example can be seen on the Radiant Ribbons cake. To create the centre for this flower, make an additional small petal and stick the resulting cone in the centre. Next, cut and colour stripes of edible (rice) paper: the width of the paper will determine the size of the centre. Repeatedly cut into the strips with scissors and steam to curl (see Success with Steam). Paint piping gel along the uncut edge of each strip and then roll up the strips like a bandage until the centre is the size you require. Finally, attach in place in the central cone with piping gel.

# Dahlia

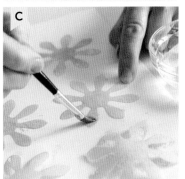

## USEFUL SPARES

It's always useful to punch out a few spare flowers to experiment with.

Simple to create with the right punch, this steam-shaped three-dimensional dahlia is very attractive, either on its own or teamed up with other flowers to create a beautiful bouquet.

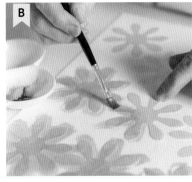

## YOU WILL NEED

- ★ 7.5cm (3in) eight-petal flower punch
- ★ yellow edible wafer (rice) paper
- ★ white paper
- ★ matt yellow food colour dust (SK Sunflower)
- ★ vegetable oil, e.g. sunflower
- ★ paintbrushes
- ★ piping gel
- ★ source of steam

## CREATING THE DAHLIA

**1.** Slide the back off your punch then, keeping it upside down, slide up to four stacked sheets of yellow edible paper into it. Firmly squeeze the handle on the punch closed to cut out a flower shape from each sheet **(A)**. The number of flowers you can cut cleanly at once will depend on the cutting edge of your punch.

**2.** Carefully remove the punch, taking care not to get any remaining paper stuck inside it. Reposition the punch as close as you can to the first flower, so as not to waste paper, and punch out as before. Continue until you have nine punched flowers for each dahlia.

**3.** Place the edible paper flowers on a clean sheet of white paper. Mix a small amount of the yellow food colour dust with a little vegetable oil to create an oil-based paint and use this to paint both sides of each flower **(B)** (see Painting on Edible Paper). Transfer the painted flowers with their textured side uppermost onto a fresh sheet of white paper and allow to dry.

**4.** Once the oil-based paint has dried, paint over the whole of each flower with piping gel **(C)**.

**5.** To shape the petals, you will need a steady source of steam (see Shaping the Paper). Pick up one of the gelled flowers and hold half the petals, with their gel side uppermost, over the steam. As the petals start to

**STICKY SITUATION**

If your gelled flowers get stuck to the white paper, simply place the underside of the paper over the steam to gently release them.

move and take on a life of their own, remove them from the steam and pinch the sides of each softened petal to give it a cupped appearance **(D)**.

**6.** Repeat this process for three more flowers. For the remaining five flowers, you will need to set the petals so that they stand up. Do this by first cupping each petal as before, then gathering the petals in your fingers **(E)**. Place the centre of the flower over the steam for a few seconds, remove from the steam and hold the flower for a few more seconds to set the petals in place. The amount that the petals need to stand up will depend upon their position in the completed flower, see **(F)** for guidance. The petals of the central flower should overlap to create a cone.

**7.** Using piping gel as a glue, stick your nine prepared flowers together, one on top of another, staggering the petals as you go **(G)**. Leave to dry completely before adding the blooms to your decorated cake.

# Chrysanthemum

Created in a similar way to the dahlia, this chrysanthemum is cut out with a punch and shaped by steam.

## YOU WILL NEED

★ eight-petal flower punches: 7.5cm (3in); 5cm (2in)

★ orange edible wafer (rice) paper

★ white paper

★ orange food colour dust (SK Berberis)

★ vegetable oil, e.g. sunflower

★ paintbrushes

★ piping gel

★ source of steam

## CREATING THE CHRYSANTHEMUM

**1.** Using up to four sheets of edible paper at once, punch out four large and three medium flowers for each chrysanthemum **(A)**.

**2.** Place the edible paper flowers onto a clean sheet of white paper. Mix a small amount of the orange food colour dust with a little vegetable oil to create an oil-based paint. Use this to paint both sides of each flower **(B)**. Transfer the painted flowers, with their textured side uppermost, onto a clean sheet of white paper and allow to dry.

**3.** Paint over the whole of each flower with piping gel **(C)**. The added moisture will make the flower centres pop up away from the paper – this is perfectly normal.

**4.** To shape the petals, you will need a steady source of steam (see Shaping the Paper). Pick up one of the gelled flowers and hold half of the petals, gel side uppermost, over the steam. The petals will start to move, curl and take on a life of their own. At this point, remove them from the steam and encourage them to curl towards the centre **(D)**. Repeat until all the petals are curled. If you are unhappy with the shape of any petal, simply place it back under the steam to reshape it.

**5.** Repeat this process for all the flowers. Then, using piping gel as a glue, stick your prepared flowers together, one on top of another. Start with the larger flowers and stagger the petals as you go **(E)**. Leave to dry completely before adding to your decorated cake.

# Spiral flower

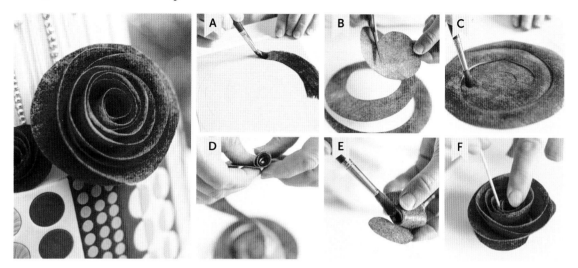

This is an easy flower to create, so it is an excellent choice for beginners. The size of your circle determines the size of your flower: the smaller the circle you use, the smaller the flower will be. However, I suggest you practise making larger flowers before attempting the smaller, more fiddly ones.

## YOU WILL NEED

★ pink edible wafer (rice) paper

★ white paper

★ large circle to draw around, e.g. plate or cake board

★ matt pink food colour dust (SK Rose)

★ vegetable oil, e.g. sunflower

★ paintbrushes

★ scissors

★ piping gel

★ cocktail stick (toothpick)

## CREATING THE SPIRAL FLOWER

**1.** Place the pink edible paper onto a sheet of white paper and draw around a large circle onto the edible paper. Starting in the centre, draw an even spiral, as shown in **(A)**. A looser spiral will make a deeper flower; a tighter spiral will make a shallower, but fuller, flower.

**2.** Mix a little of the dust with a small amount of vegetable oil to create an oil-based paint (see Painting on Edible Paper). Use this to paint both sides of the edible paper circle **(A)**. Transfer the circle onto a fresh sheet of white paper and allow to dry.

**3.** When dry, start at the outside edge and use a pair of scissors to cut along the drawn spiral line into the centre **(B)**.

**4.** Place the spiral, with its textured side uppermost, onto a clean sheet of white paper. Lightly paint over the spiral with piping gel **(C)**.

**5.** Roll up your flower as soon as you have applied the piping gel to prevent the paper becoming too soft and tearing. Pick up the outside edge of the spiral and start to roll it like a bandage, with the textured, gelled side of the paper on the inside of the roll **(D)**. Roll tightly at first but then allow the flower to open up by rolling more and more loosely. Continue rolling until you come to the centre.

**6.** Paint piping gel over the base of the roll **(E)**, then place it onto the centre. The spiral will probably open up a little more at this point, a little like a spring. Use a cocktail stick to adjust the distribution of the coils and open up the centre a little more if required **(F)**. Leave to set.

**7.** Once set, you can easily trim off sections of the spiral with scissors to even up the appearance of the flower.

# Carnation

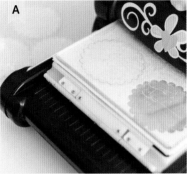

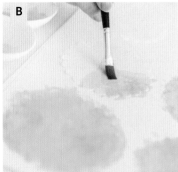

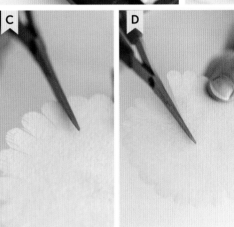

*T*he scalloped circles on the carnation are made using a die-cutting machine. Dies and die-cutting machines are widely used by papercrafters; they are easy to store and can be more economical than buying multiple punches. If you don't own a die-cutting machine, I suggest that you borrow one to begin with.

## YOU WILL NEED

- ★ white edible wafer (rice) paper
- ★ die-cutting machine
- ★ 8cm (3¼in) classic scalloped circle die
- ★ white paper
- ★ matt lime green food colour dust (SK Vine)
- ★ vegetable oil, e.g. sunflower
- ★ paintbrushes
- ★ scissors
- ★ piping gel
- ★ source of steam

## CREATING THE CARNATION

**1.** Cut sheets of edible paper to fit your die-cutter plates. Follow the manufacturer's instructions to set up the die cutter with the edible paper and die. Turn the handle to cut out the scalloped circles: I cut four at once. Reposition the die and repeat **(A)** – you will need five or six circles for each carnation.

**2.** Place the scalloped circles onto a clean sheet of white paper. Mix a small amount of food colour dust with a little vegetable oil to create an oil-based paint (see Painting on Edible Paper). Paint both sides of each circle **(B)**, then transfer the painted circles with their textured side uppermost onto a fresh sheet of white paper. Leave to dry.

**3.** Once dry, take a small pair of scissors and make repeated 5–6mm (¼in) deep cuts around the scallop edges, increasing this to 1cm (⅜in) deep cuts where the scallops meet **(C)**.

**4.** Take one of the circles and cut into the centre **(D)** – this will form the outside edges of the flower later.

**5.** Paint over each flower completely with piping gel **(E)**.

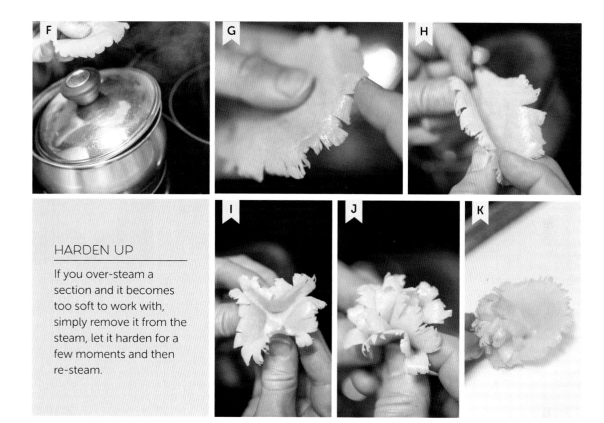

## HARDEN UP

If you over-steam a section and it becomes too soft to work with, simply remove it from the steam, let it harden for a few moments and then re-steam.

**6.** To shape and build the carnation you will need a steady source of steam (see Shaping the Paper). Pick up one of the gelled flowers, holding the gel side uppermost. Place part of the scalloped edges over the steam and, as the paper starts to move **(F)**, remove it from the steam. Use a finger to quickly separate the cuts around the edges of the steamed scallops to create a frilled edge **(G)**. Repeat until you have frilled all the scallops. Repeat this process for four or five more scalloped circles.

**7.** Pick up the scalloped circle with the central cut then, using piping gel as a glue, overlap the two cut edges by approximately 3.5cm (1⅜in) to create a cone.

**8.** Next, place the centre of one of the frilled scalloped circles over the steam to soften it. Remove from the steam and fold in half across the centre, as shown **(H)**. Replace back into the steam to re-soften, if necessary, and push the folded ends together to form a cross shape **(I)**. Next, re-soften and wrap the points of the cross around to create a rough circular shape **(J)**.

**9.** Paint piping gel onto the back of the shaped scallop and place it inside the cone made earlier **(K)**. Repeat, adding enough frilled and shaped scallops to completely fill the cone. Leave to dry completely before adding to your decorated cake.

# Hybrid musk rose

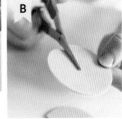

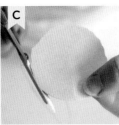

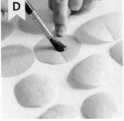

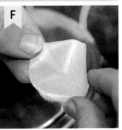

*I* have chosen to create this exquisitely scented, wonderfully soft and feminine shrub rose from my garden at the point just before all the petals unfurl to reveal the central stamens. This is the most challenging flower in this chapter so be patient, take your time, work in stages and be prepared to get a little sticky!

## YOU WILL NEED

★ edible wafer (rice) paper: pink; green

★ circle punches: 6.5cm (2½in); 5cm (2in); 4cm (1½in)

★ scissors

★ white paper

★ paintbrushes

★ piping gel

★ source of steam

★ 22-gauge white floristry wire

★ 2.5cm (1in) polystyrene ball

★ 10g (¼oz) pale green sugarpaste (rolled fondant)

★ Dresden tool

## CREATING THE HYBRID MUSK ROSE

**1.** Using edible pink paper, punch out circles or cut them out using scissors **(A)**. The number of circles you need will depend on how full or tight you would like your rose to appear. To make the rose shown you will need approximately 8 small, 11 medium and 20 large circles.

**2.** Holding up to four circles together, cut into the centre of each circle with scissors **(B)**.

**3.** Holding two or three circles at a time, cut into each edge a little to shape them **(C)**. Add splits and jagged sections too, as flowers are never perfect.

**4.** Place all the petals, textured side up, on white paper. Paint over them with piping gel **(D)**.

**5.** To make the small petals, leave four petals flat and cup the remainder with the gel side innermost, by overlapping the cut edges to create shallow cones **(E)**. Leave to dry.

**6.** Cup the medium and large petals, overlapping the petals so the gelled side is on the outside of the petal and the smooth side of the paper is in the centre of the cup. Leave to dry.

**7.** To give the petals movement you will need a steady source of steam (see Shaping the Paper). Start with the large petals, as these are easier to handle. Pick up a gelled petal and hold it on the join with the gel side towards the steam. Then place the outer edge of the petal over the steam to gently soften the paper. Too little steam and the paper won't curl; too much and the paper starts to buckle!

**8.** Remove the petal from the steam and test: if the paper easily curls when you press on it with a finger, quickly curl the edges of the petal backwards away from the cup **(F)**. If the paper doesn't move sufficiently, place it back under the steam, then test again. The shapes of each petal should be different: some should have one curl and

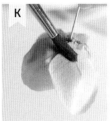

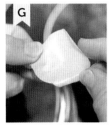

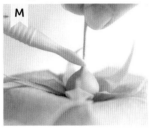

## QUICK DRY

Dry the rose in a cool 50–60°C (122–140°F) oven for a few minutes.

some two. Repeat for all the remaining large petals.

**9.** Steam and curl the medium petals, this time making a few that curl inwards as well as outwards **(G)**. The side you steam will determine the direction of the curl; paper naturally curls towards steam.

**10.** Steam the small petals and slightly curl outwards, but only a fraction along their edges – this is very subtle.

**11.** Insert the floristry wire into the polystyrene ball and secure firmly in place with glue. Place one of the small flat petals, gel side down, over the top of the ball. Use a damp paintbrush to shape the paper around the ball **(H)**. You will in effect be melting the paper with the water. If you add too much water the petals start to slip and slide: if this happens dry the rose (see tip) before adding any more petals.

**12.** Place the second petal with its gel side against the ball, so the tip is at the top of the ball

and the base is against the wire. Use a damp paintbrush to shape the paper around the ball. Add two more petals that also meet at the top to create the rose centre **(I)**.

**13.** Add the second layer to the rose, using the remaining small cupped petals. Place the first petal over a join in the first row **(J)**, then overlap the remaining petals around the centre, again, using the damp paintbrush to help stick and mould them into position.

**14.** Add two overlapping rows of medium petals **(K)**. Note that the centre of a rose is usually flat, so try and keep all the petals at similar height to the first two rows. Next, add rows of the largest petals, allowing them to gradually fall outwards to create a rose about to come into full bloom. Set aside.

**15.** For the calyx, use scissors to cut out five 4cm (1½in) long truncated teardrop shapes from green edible paper. Gel and cup

the larger end of the teardrops, as for the petals, then gently steam the tips to curl and attach to the back of the rose as shown **(L)**.

**16.** For the hip, roll a 1.3cm (½in) wide ball of pale green sugarpaste. Thread it centrally onto the wire and down to meet the calyx. Use a Dresden tool to blend the base of the hip into the paper covering of the wire **(M)**.

# WEDDING CAKE BASICS

A wedding cake is usually something you undertake once you are a competent baker and have at least a little experience of cake decorating. For this reason, I am going to quickly skim over a few basics. However, if you are relatively new to cake decorating – and I know some people do take on wedding cake projects with little experience – I would urge you to refer to my earlier books or my blog for recipes and advice.

### PERFECT RECIPES

Find delicious cake recipes, suitable for decorating, in many of Lindy's previous books and in the recipe section of the Lindy's Cakes blog.

## PREPARATION AND PLANNING

A wedding cake – especially if it is your first – can be a huge undertaking, so plan well in advance and try not to leave everything to the last minute. Here are some useful planning suggestions:

**1.** Buy in all your specialist equipment and ingredients as soon as you've chosen your design.

**2.** Make any decorations that can be created in advance, such as edible lace or wafer (rice) paper flowers, and store them carefully.

**3.** Experiment with unfamiliar techniques – practise makes perfect! This will give you more confidence when it comes to decorating the cake.

**4.** Choose the cake recipes you will be using and experiment with practise bakes if you feel unsure.

**5.** Write a baking and decorating timetable: I find projects are less daunting if I have a clear plan.

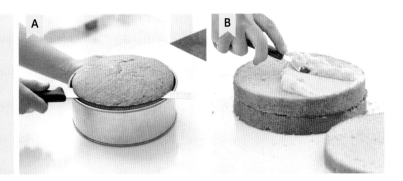

# CHOOSING AND BAKING CAKES

It's important to select a recipe that not only tastes wonderful, but also supports the sugarpaste (rolled fondant) and decorations: I recommend chocolate fudge cake, flavoured Madeira or a traditional fruit cake. By all means be more adventurous, but remember that it's easier to decorate a firmer cake, and the longer a cake stays fresh, the more time you have to decorate it. You can also create tiers with cake dummies and use cutting cakes behind the scenes.

# DECORATING MATERIALS

Before you can begin to decorate you will need a selection of edible materials, such as sugarpaste, modelling paste, buttercream and royal icing. You can either buy these from specialist suppliers or make them yourself. I personally buy in professional sugarpaste and marzipan, but make everything else myself – the choice is yours. Recipes to make your own can be found in my many cake-decorating books or on my blog.

I have used two types of commercially available sugarpaste to complete the projects; both have different properties and work well together. I have used M&B sugarpaste, which is a lovely soft paste that I find easy to work with and is excellent for making modelling paste. For the tall cakes and cakes with sharp edges that are covered at once, I used the beautiful, smooth and silky Massa Ticino sugarpaste: a much firmer paste that enables you to be more adventurous with your covering.

# LEVELLING CAKES

Making an accurate level cake base is an important part of creating your masterpiece. Here are two ways of doing this:

## USING A SET SQUARE

Place a set square up against the edge of the cake and use a sharp knife to mark a line around the top of the cake at the required height. With a large serrated knife, cut around the marked line and across the cake to remove the domed crust.

## USING A TIN

Place a cake board into the base of the tin (pan) in which your cake was baked, so that when the cake is placed on top, the outer edge of the cake is level with the tin. Take a long, sharp knife and cut the dome from the cake, keeping the knife against the tin **(A)**. This will ensure the cake is completely level.

# FILLING CAKES

It is not always necessary to add fillings to cakes, however, many people like to fill their cakes with complementary flavours, such as chocolate and orange ganache, praline buttercream or delicious homemade lemon curd.

To do this, split the cake into a number of horizontal layers and spread each layer with the filling(s) **(B)**, setting it in the fridge if appropriate. When choosing fillings, bear in mind that your cakes have to support the weight of the sugarpaste and decoration, so thin layers or layers that set firm are preferable.

# ADDING A BASE LAYER

To help you achieve a perfectly smooth finish to your sugarpasted (rolled fondant) cake, you will need to cover the cake with a base layer of buttercream, ganache or marzipan, depending on personal choice and the finished look you are planning to create.

## COVERING WITH BUTTERCREAM

A buttercream covering, or crumb coat, is the traditional way to prepare a sponge cake to be sugarpasted. The buttercream layer helps to create an even surface and seal in the crumbs. Apply the buttercream just before covering a cake with sugarpaste so that it acts as a glue.

**1.** Place the cake on a board of the same size, using a little buttercream.

**2.** Beat your buttercream until it has a soft and spreadable consistency.

**3.** Using a palette knife, cover the cake with a thin layer of buttercream, filling any holes and creating a smooth surface for the sugarpaste layer **(A)**.

## COVERING WITH GANACHE

Chocolate ganache is a delicious alternative, especially when paired with chocolate cake. It sets firm, adding stability to cakes, making them easier to cover. It is also useful if you want to achieve sharp edges. Ganache takes a little longer to apply as the two layers need to set. Use a white chocolate ganache for cakes to be covered with a light-coloured sugarpaste.

**1.** Make the ganache, following the recipe on the Lindy's Cakes blog, and allow it to set.

**2.** Mix and soften the ganache until it is smooth and easy to spread. If your ganache is hard, place it in a microwave for a few seconds at a time to soften it.

**3.** Use a little ganache to attach the cake to a board of the same size. Place in a freezer for a few minutes to set.

**4.** Use a palette knife to roughly cover the top and sides of the cake with a thick layer of ganache, making sure there are no air pockets **(B)**.

**5.** Take off the excess with a side scraper or set square **(C)**, bringing in the excess ganache from the top edge onto the top of the cake. Place in a freezer for a few minutes to set.

**6.** Add a second layer, ensuring that the finish is perfectly smooth, the cake sides are vertical and the top is level **(D)**. Set in a freezer.

**7.** To attach sugarpaste simply brush hot water, sugar syrup (flavoured if desired) or piping gel over the ganached cake to act as a glue.

## CORNFLOUR FREE

Don't use icing (confectioners') sugar with added cornflour (cornstarch) to roll out your marzipan; the presence of cornflour may cause fermentation.

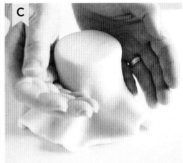

## COVERING WITH MARZIPAN

A fruit cake should be covered with marzipan before the sugarpaste covering is applied: to add flavour, to seal in moisture and to prevent the fruit staining the sugarpaste. For best results, choose a white marzipan with a smooth texture and a high almond content (at least 23.5 per cent).

**1.** Unwrap the cake and roll over the top with a rolling pin to flatten it slightly. If the cake is to sit on a silver foil-covered cake board, cover the top of the board with a very thin layer of marzipan, then roll over this with a rolling pin. This will prevent the acid in the fruit from dissolving the silver covering of the board – important if the cake is going to be kept for any length of time once covered.

**2.** Turn the cake over so that the flatter surface (the base) becomes the top and place it on greaseproof (wax) paper.

**3.** Knead the marzipan so that it becomes supple; do not over-knead, as this releases oils from the marzipan and changes its consistency.

**4.** Brush warm apricot glaze into the gap around the base. Roll a long sausage of marzipan and wrap it around the base. Use a smoother to press it under the cake to fill any gaps.

**5.** Brush the cake with warm apricot glaze **(A)** and use small pieces of marzipan to fill in any holes. Roll out the marzipan between 5mm (¼in) spacers, using icing (confectioners') sugar or white vegetable fat (shortening) to stop it sticking to your work surface. Turn the marzipan around while rolling to maintain an appropriate shape, but do not turn it over.

**6.** Lift up the marzipan over a rolling pin and place it over the cake **(B)**. Smooth the top of the cake with a smoother to remove any air bubbles, and then gently ease the marzipan down the sides of the cake into position, making sure there are no pleats. Smooth the top curved edge with the palm of your hand **(C)** and the sides with a smoother.

**7.** Use a smoother to gradually press down around the edge of the cake into the excess marzipan. Trim to create a neat edge. Allow the marzipan to harden in a warm, dry place for 24–48 hours before decorating the cake, so the base is firm.

**8.** To attach sugarpaste to a marzipan-covered cake simply moisten the surface of the marzipan with a clear spirit, such as gin or vodka. Coat evenly to prevent air bubbles forming under the sugarpaste.

# COVERING CAKES WITH SUGARPASTE

There are a variety of ways to cover a cake with sugarpaste (rolled fondant); the height of the cake, the shape of the top edge and the decoration will determine which is most appropriate from the following methods:

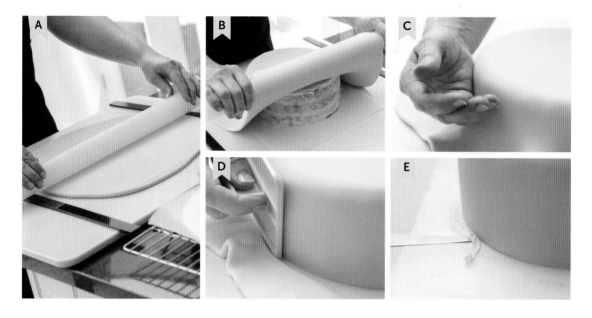

## REGULAR CAKES

These cakes are usually up to 10cm (4in) in height.

### METHOD 1: STANDARD

This technique gives a smooth, rounded finish to the top edge of a cake.

**1.** Knead the sugarpaste until warm and pliable. Roll out to a 5mm (¼in) depth on a non-stick mat or surface lightly smeared with white vegetable fat (shortening), rather than icing (confectioners') sugar. Use spacers to ensure an even thickness **(A)**.

**2.** Lift the paste carefully over the top of the cake, support it with a rolling pin and position it so that it covers the cake **(B)**.

Use a smoother to smooth the top surface of the cake to remove any lumps, then smooth the top edge with the palm of your hand.

**3.** Using a cupped hand and an upward movement, encourage the sugarpaste on the sides to adjust to the shape of your cake **(C)**. Do not press down on any pleats in the paste; instead open them out and redistribute the paste until the cake is completely covered. Smooth the sides using a smoother.

**4.** Take the smoother and, while pressing down, run the flat edge around the base of the cake to create a cutting line **(D)**. Trim away the excess paste with a palette knife to create a neat edge **(E)**.

## METHOD 2: SHARP EDGE

This is a slight adaptation of Method 1 that gives the edges a sharper finish. The trick is to use a firm chocolate ganache base layer (see Covering with Ganache), a thinner layer of sugarpaste and a pair of flexi smoothers. It's also important to allow yourself time to work on achieving the sharp edges!

**1.** Roll out your sugarpaste to a depth of 4mm (⅛in); slightly thinner than in Method 1.

**2.** Cover your cake, following Method 1. Place the rounded-edged flexi smoother on top of your cake, matching the curve of the smoother with the edge of your cake. Position the rectangular smoother on the side of your cake.

## CLEAN FINISH

Always make sure your hands are clean and dry with no traces of cake crumbs before smoothing sugarpaste.

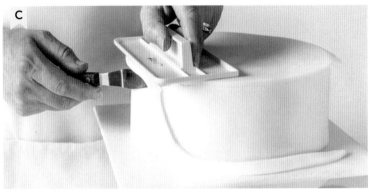

## POP THE BUBBLES

If you find you have unwanted air bubbles under the icing, insert a scriber or a clean dressmakers' pin at an angle to press out the air.

**3.** Use medium pressure to rub the rectangular smoother around the side of the cake, while pressing on the top smoother at the same time. You should quickly see the sharp edge appear.

**4.** Continue to work around your cake in this way until you are happy with the finish.

### METHOD 3: VERY SHARP EDGE (TWO PIECE)

This is a fantastic technique for creating very sharp edges. As two pieces of paste are used there will be a join, so think carefully about whether to have this on the top or side of your cake. For example, the join on the base tier of the Retro Circle cake is on the side, as it is covered by the decoration; therefore the sides are covered first, followed by the top.

### THE SIDES

**1.** Knead the sugarpaste until it is warm, then roll it into a sausage shape with its length equalling the circumference of the cake. Place the sausage on your work surface and roll over it to widen the paste to at least the height of the cake and a thickness of 5mm (¼in). Cut one edge straight.

**2.** Cover the sides with a thin layer of buttercream. Carefully roll up the sugarpaste like a bandage, then unroll it around the sides of the cake so the cut edge of the sugarpaste is flush with the lower edge of the cake **(A)**. Smooth the paste with a smoother to give an even surface. If necessary, roughly cut away any excess paste with scissors, to remove the excess weight rather than to give a neat finish.

**3.** Place the smoother onto the sugarpaste surface so it partially rests above the edge of the cake. Use a palette knife to remove the excess paste by cutting away from the cake onto the smoother **(B)**.

### THE TOP

**1.** Roll out more sugarpaste to 5mm (¼in) thick and use it to cover the top, roughly cutting away the excess paste with scissors.

**2.** Place the smoother onto the sugarpaste surface so that it slightly overhangs the edge of the cake. Use a palette knife to remove the excess paste by cutting away from the cake onto the smoother **(C)**.

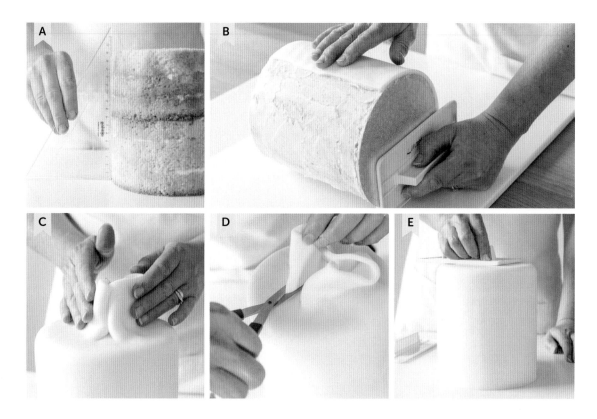

## TALL CAKES

Once a cake reaches a certain height it becomes no longer possible to cover it using the three methods for regular cakes. Opt for one of the two methods below, depending on whether you want curved or sharp edges.

### METHOD 4: ROLLING AND FOLDING FOR TALL CAKES

Use this method to cover a cake with curved edges. It's important to check the sides of your tall cake are all vertical before you begin to cover it.

**1.** Measure the circumference and height of your cake using a set square **(A)**, then cover it with buttercream (see Covering with Buttercream).

**2.** Knead the sugarpaste to warm it, then roll it out into a rectangular shape between 5mm (¼in) spacers. Turn the paste over and cut it into a rectangle: the length needs to be slightly longer than the circumference of your cake and the width should measure the height plus the radius. Place a board under the cake, then position the cake onto its side on the sugarpaste rectangle so the base is flush with one long edge **(B)**. Roll the cake up in the paste, trim as necessary with a palette or craft knife to create a neat, straight join and rub the join closed using the heat of your hand.

**3.** Stand your cake upright on greaseproof (wax) paper, fold the sugarpaste over the top of the cake and smooth in the paste as far as you can by hand **(C)**. Cut away the excess paste using scissors **(D)**. Finally, use a smoother to smooth the sides and top of the cake **(E)**.

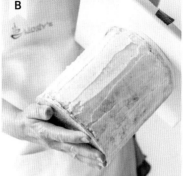

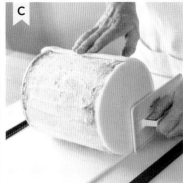

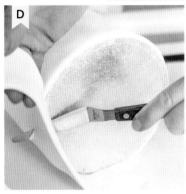

## DISGUISE THE JOIN

The join in the sugarpaste is usually disguised by the decoration, but if not you can simply add a string of pearls or sugar ribbon to give it a neat finish.

## METHOD 5: VERY SHARP EDGE (TWO PIECE) FOR TALL CAKES

This method is done in two stages, as the top and sides are covered separately. Whether you cover the top or the sides first will depend on the decoration. I usually apply the top first, as described below, but please refer to each project for guidance.

**1.** Place your buttercream- or ganache-covered cake on a cake board of the same size. Roll out a disc of sugarpaste, larger than the top of your cake, turn the paste over and place it on a cake board covered with greaseproof (wax) paper.

**2.** Turn your cake upside down and place it onto the sugarpaste. Use a palette knife to cut around the edge of the cake, cutting down into the sugarpaste **(A)**.

**3.** Use the two boards to help you turn your cake upright **(B)**.

**4.** Roll out the sugarpaste into a large rectangular shape using 5mm (¼in) spacers. Turn the paste over and cut it into a rectangle: the length needs to be slightly longer than the circumference and the width should be the same as the height of the cake. Position the cake on its side onto the paste, so the covered top is flush with one long edge. Roll the cake

up in the sugarpaste, using a smoother to guide you **(C)**.

**5.** Trim the paste as necessary using a palette or craft knife to create a neat straight join, and rub the join closed with the heat of your hand.

**6.** Finally, use a palette knife to cut away the excess sugarpaste from the base **(D)**, then stand the cake upright.

## BALL CAKES

I used a ball cake to add interest to my Retro Circles cake; recipes for making these can be found on my blog or in my previous titles. When covering a ball cake, plan where to position your pleats so that they can be easily covered with the decoration. Take your time when smoothing them; the paste will not dry out if you continually work it.

**1.** Place the ball cake on greaseproof (wax) paper and cover with buttercream or marzipan (see Adding a Base Layer). Using spacers, roll out some sugarpaste to a 5mm (¼in) thickness, ideally into a circle the same diameter as the circumference of your cake.

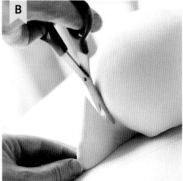

Place the paste over the ball cake and ease it around the base using the palm of your hand, pulling up the excess to form two or more pleats **(A)**.

**2.** Cut the pleats away with scissors **(B)** and smooth the joins closed – they should disappear quite quickly with the heat of your hand. Trim any excess paste away from the base of the cake using a palette knife. Using a smoother followed by your hand, smooth the surface of the cake with vertical strokes. Set the cake aside to dry.

## COVERING BOARDS

Covering the board adds a professional touch to your design.

**1.** Roll out the sugarpaste to a depth of 5mm (¼in), ideally using spacers.

**2.** Moisten the board with water or sugar glue. Lift up the paste and drape it over the board **(A)**.

**3.** Circle a smoother over the paste to achieve a smooth, flat finish to the board **(B)**.

**4.** Cut the paste flush with the sides of the board using a cranked handled palette knife, taking care to keep the edge vertical **(C)**. The covered board should ideally be left overnight to dry thoroughly.

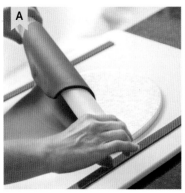

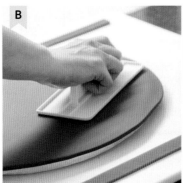

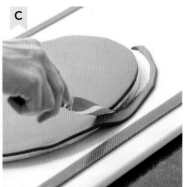

# CAKE CONSTRUCTION

A multi-tiered cake, like a building, needs a structure hidden within it to prevent it from collapsing. It is important that this structure is 'built' correctly to take the loads put upon it, so please follow the instructions carefully, as it is worth the time involved to get this stage correct.

## DOWELLING CAKES

All but the top cake will usually need dowelling to provide support. It is essential that all the dowels are inserted vertically, are the same length and have flat tops, and also that all the cakes being stacked have hardboards beneath them.

**1.** To dowel a cake, centre a cake board the same size as the tier above and score around the edge of the board with a scriber to leave a visible outline **(A)**.

**2.** Insert a dowel 2.5cm (1in) in from the scored line, vertically down through the cake to the cake board below. Make a knife

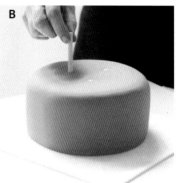

scratch or pencil mark on the dowel to mark the exact height, then remove the dowel.

**3.** Take a sharp cutter and cut cleanly across the dowel, using the pencil mark to guide you.

**4.** Cut two or more dowels to the same length. Place the first back into the measuring hole and insert the other dowels at even spaces within the scribed circle **(B)**. Repeat for all but the top cake.

## STACKING CAKES

Cover and dowel each cake before carefully stacking them using the following method:

**1.** Check that each cake is level using a spirit level and spare cake board **(A)**.

**2.** Use a palette knife to spread 15ml (1 tbsp) of royal icing within the scribed area on the base cake, covering the dowels **(B)**.

**3.** Place the next sized cake on top using the scored line as a placement guide.

**4.** Use a set square to check the placement of the cake, adjusting the positioning while the royal icing is still wet **(C)**. Repeat for the remaining cakes.

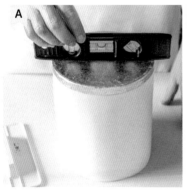

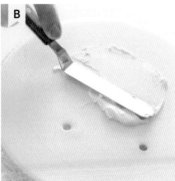

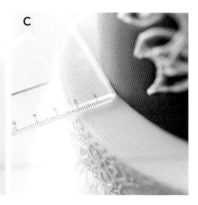

# STORAGE AND TRANSPORTATION

The following conditions will adversely affect your decorated cakes:

**Sunlight** will fade and alter the colours of the icing, so always store your cake in a dark place.

**Humidity** can have a disastrous effect on decorations, causing the icing to become soft and to droop if free standing. It can also cause dark colours to bleed into lighter colours and silver decorations to tarnish.

**Heat** can melt icing, especially buttercream, and prevent sugarpaste from crusting over.

It is therefore best to protect your decorated cake as much as possible. Store your completed cake in a covered cardboard cake box, placing it somewhere cool and dry – not in a refrigerator. If the box is slightly larger than the cake and it is to be transported, use non-slip matting to prevent the cake from moving. If the weather is humid, use a dehumidifier and transport only in an air-conditioned vehicle, if possible.

# CUTTING THE CAKE

Although this is usually done by venue staff or caterers, I am often asked about how to divide and cut a wedding cake. The secret to success is to cut the cake into squares or rectangles, rather than pie slices. There are various ways of doing this, but here is a very easy option. Start by deconstructing the tiers and removing the dowels. Use a sharp pastry knife to cut across the centre of the cake first, and then cut parallel lines 2.5cm (1in) apart. Next, cut a perpendicular line through the centre, followed by parallel lines of the required width: 5cm (2in) for sponge cakes and 2.5cm (1in) for fruit cakes.

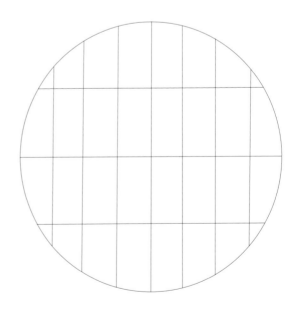

## COMPANY ABBREVIATIONS USED IN THIS BOOK

**DS** – Designer Stencils
**FI** – First Impressions
**FMM** – FMM Sugarcraft
**HP** – Holly products
**KD** – Karen Davies
**KT** – Kemper Tools
**LC** – Lindy's Cakes Ltd
**MM** – Marvelous Molds
**MT** – Massa Ticino
**PC** – Patchwork Cutters
**PME** – PME Sugarcraft
**SK** – Squires Kitchen
**SF** – Sugarflair
**SM** – Silikomart

# Sponsors

## SPECIALIST CUTTERS, COOKIE CUTTERS AND STENCILS:

**Lindy's Cakes Ltd (LC)**
Brandhill, Onibury
Craven Arms
Shropshire  SY7 0PG
www.lindyscakes.co.uk

## SUGARPASTE

**Massa Ticino (MT)**
Carma®/Barry Callebaut Schweiz
Ag
Pfingstweidstrasse 60
8005 Zurich
Switzerland
www.carma.ch

**M&B of London**
3a Milmead Industrial Estate
Mill Mead Road
London N17 9QU
www.mbsc.co.uk

## ONLAYS

**Marvelous molds**
7609 Production Drive
Cincinnati
OH 45237
United States
www.marvelousmolds.com

# Picture Credits

**Dreaming and Planning**
*Pink Bouquet:* kireewong foto/
Shutterstock.com
**Setting the Scene**
*Table setting at a luxury wedding reception:* Dallas Events Inc/
Shutterstock.com
**Sweetheart Stripes**
*Red Dahlia Flower:* Suwat
Wongkham/Shutterstock.com
*Heart Shaped Macaroons:*
Nana77777/Shutterstock.com
*Pink Accents on a Summer Tuxedo:*
Maria Dryfhout/Shutterstock.com
*Seating Arrangement:* Mejini
Neskah/Shutterstock.com
**Something Blue**
*Blue Bouquet:* Nathalie
Photography/Shutterstock.com
*Bride and Groom on Wooden
Bridge:* Andrei Zveaghintev/
Shutterstock.com

**Retro Circles**
*Floral Arrangement at a Beach
Ceremony:* wandee007/
Shutterstock.com
*Pearl Necklace on White
Background:* Maya Kruchankova/
Shutterstock.com
**Flamboyant Fleur-de-lis**
*Row of Bridesmaids with Flowers:*
Karen Grigoryan/Shutterstock.com
*Wedding Car with White Ribbons:*
MNStudio/Shutterstock.com
**Designer Doodle Art**
*Pink rose boutonniere flower on
groom's wedding coat:* aastock/
Shutterstock.com
*Wedding table setting:* Shebeko/
Shutterstock.com
*Beautiful Table Setting:* Daria
Minaeva/Shutterstock.com

**Fabulous Fringes**
*Bride and Bridesmaids Show
off their Shoes:* MNStudio/
Shutterstock.com
*White Peonies in Floral Vase:*
Mila May/Shutterstock.com
**Bridal Vogue**
*Purple Shoes in a Bride's Hand:*
Alex Andrei/Shutterstock.com
*Wedding Table with Number Eight:*
c12/Shutterstock.com
*Decoration of a chair on a wedding
banquet at restaurant. Gentle
peach rose:* Nadiia Balytska/
Shutterstock.com
**Glitz and Glamour**
*Beautiful Silver Background with
Wedding Rings and Stars:* Gudrun
Muenz/Shutterstock.com
*Line Up of Top Hats:* Gordon Ball
LRPS/Shutterstock.com
*Wedding Shoes and Dress:* Karen
Grigoryan/Shutterstock.com

# About the Author

Well known and highly respected in the cake decorating industry, Lindy Smith has over 25 years experience in sugarcraft. A former chartered surveyor, Lindy was originally inspired to start cake decorating by her own wedding cake. Lindy is a cake designer who not only creates amazing edible creations, but also loves to share her passion for sugarcraft and inspire fellow enthusiasts. She is the author of 15 cake decorating titles, 13 of these being for D&C; the most recent including *Lindy Smith's Mini Cakes Academy*, *Creative Colour for Cake Decorating*, which won an International Gourmand Cookbook award for Best Pastry Sweet Book in the UK in 2014, and her internationally best-selling *The Contemporary Cake Decorating Bible*.

Lindy has appeared on television many times, most recently on *Create & Craft TV*, but she has also appeared on programmes such as BBC1's *Generation Game* and presented a sugarcraft series for *Good Food Live*. Lindy loves to teach and has travelled to many parts of the globe to share her skills and knowledge through hands-on classes and demonstrations, both large and small. She also teaches online via the Craftsy platform.

Lindy's cake mission is to inspire and bring a fresh contemporary look to sugarcraft design. Her well-established company Lindy's Cakes Ltd supplies, via its online shop, quality cake-decorating products including Lindy's own ranges of sugarcraft cutters, cookie cutters and cake decorating stencils.

In 2012, Lindy won *Insight Magazine*'s Business Woman of the Year title. Katherine Benson, the editor said: "Lindy Smith is a remarkable woman. Not only does she boast high level skills to create her own designs, but she thrives on helping others achieve their goals when it comes to making that cake not only taste good, but look good too. Her range of knowledge is extensive and from her website to her books, cutters and stencils and classes, Lindy has shown that being business savvy isn't all about profiting yourself, but also about profiting others too."

To see what Lindy is currently doing, become a fan of Lindy's Cakes on Facebook or follow Lindy on Twitter and Pinterest. For baking advice and a wealth of information, visit her blog via the Lindy's Cakes website.

**www.lindyscakes.co.uk**

# Acknowledgments

Creating a book is always a time-consuming process with many steps along the way, from the initial in-depth researching and experimenting to the eventual creating, writing, photography and editing. I would therefore like to thank those who have helped me move from one step to the next. I would especially like to thank my mother for introducing me to her die-cutting machine and her many papercraft punches, and also for teaching me the basics of using these effectively.

A special mention goes to my fabulous, now grown-up children for gallantly volunteering to dress up and be photographic models. Charlotte, you make such a beautiful 'bride' and Tristan, I know that cake was heavy, so thank you for your strength in holding it steady. I'd also like to thank my husband Graham, who was given no option but to don a morning suit and became a part of this book too – it really wasn't that bad was it?

I would like to mention the generosity of both my sugarpaste suppliers. Without your wonderful pastes, covering these wedding cakes wouldn't have been so easy. I would also like to thank Marvelous Molds for supplying me with samples of their innovative Onlays, my inspiration for the Flamboyant Fleur-de-lis cake.

Thank you to Jack Kirby for yet more stunning photos, it was a pleasure working with you again. To see more of Jack's wonderful shots, take a look at my *Mini Cakes Academy* and Gourmand award-winning *Creative Colour for Cake Decorating* books. Finally, I'd like to thank the team at my publishers for allowing me a huge amount of creative freedom and for letting me develop and implement my ideas.

# Index

A DAVID & CHARLES BOOK
© F&W Media International, Ltd 2016

David & Charles is an imprint of F&W Media International, Ltd
Brunel House, Forde Close, Newton Abbot, TQ12 4PU, UK

F&W Media International, Ltd is a subsidiary of F+W Media, Inc
10151 Carver Road, Suite #200, Blue Ash, OH 45242, USA

Text and Designs © Lindy Smith 2016
Layout © F&W Media International, Ltd 2016,
Photography © F&W Media International Ltd 2016, except mood board images
© Lindy & Charlotte Smith, Bang Wallop Photography and those listed in the
Picture Credits (see p.141) © Shutterstock.

First published in the UK and USA in 2016

A catalogue record for this book is available from the British Library.

ISBN-13: 978-1-4463-0603-1 paperback
ISBN-10: 1-4463-0603-8 paperback

ISBN-13: 978-1-4463-0601-7 hardback
ISBN-10: 1-4463-0601-1 hardback

ISBN-13: 978-1-4463-7431-3 PDF
ISBN-10: 1-4463-7431-9 PDF

ISBN-13: 978-1-4463-7432-0 EPUB
ISBN-10: 1-4463-7432-7 EPUB

Printed in China by RR Donnelley for:
F&W Media International, Ltd
Brunel House, Forde Close, Newton Abbot, TQ12 4PU, UK

10 9 8 7 6 5 4 3 2 1

Content Director: Ame Verso
Project Editor: Beth Dymond
Art Editor: Anna Wade
Stylist: Lindy Smith
Photographer: Jack Kirby
Production Controller: Beverley Richardson

F+W Media publishes high quality books on a wide range of subjects.
For more great book ideas visit: www.stitchcraftcreate.co.uk

Layout of the digital edition of this book may vary depending on reader
hardware and display settings.